Adam, the Baby, and the Man from Mars

ADAM, THE BABY AND THE MAN FROM MARS

IRWIN EDMAN

Essay Index Reprint Series

BOOKS FOR LIBRARIES PRESS
FREEPORT, NEW YORK

LIBRARY OF CONGRESS CATALOG CARD NUMBER:
68-24850

PRINTED IN THE UNITED STATES OF AMERICA

PREFACE

A COLLECTION of essays is necessarily a miscellany. It consists of writings on various themes composed for diverse occasions or on random provocations. It lacks the possible integrity of form of a novel or a philosophy; it tells no single story, elucidates no single prejudice or dogma. It ranges, as do the papers that follow, from memories of Americans met in foreign countries to speculations on the nature of religion or the universe. Its language is as various as its occasions. Its parts differ from each other as do the letters one writes to one's friends.

But like the letters written to a number of friends by the same person, so do the essays written by a single writer reveal a characteristic temper, perhaps even a characteristic philosophy. I suspect that the following essays, willy-nilly, are of a piece. Their author happens to be engaged in the profession of what is commonly called philosophy. He happens likewise to be living in the twentieth century, in America, and in New York. He has been

v

educated in, or exposed to, a point of view that might roughly be called naturalism, the world that science reveals. He has a nostalgic passion for what may be called Platonism, the world that poetry remembers. The writer has likewise for ten years been within the walls of the academy. But those walls in the modern academy are thin and their open doors easily open upon the world. He has looked through and walked through those doors often. But the eyes with which he has looked have been those of a philosophy he has learned to cherish. What that philosophy, if any, is, ought to be discernible in the following pages. What objects have been regarded, these pages, if they are intelligible, ought also to reveal. Like those allegedly unprejudiced observers of the human scene, Adam, the Baby, and the Man from Mars, the writer thinks himself unprejudiced. Like them, he is not. But like theirs, his subject is the human scene. That much unity at least there is in these pages.

These papers have appeared in various journals. For permission to reprint, the author wishes to thank the editors of 'Harper's Magazine,' 'The Century Magazine,' 'The Forum,' 'Books,' 'The Bookman,' 'The Nation,' and

Preface

'The Journal of Philosophy.' For the chance to have these essays attain the permanence of a book he thanks his publishers.

I. E.

COLUMBIA UNIVERSITY
December 18, 1928

CONTENTS

ON AMERICAN LIFE

ANTIDOTES

SPECULATIONS

TOWARD A PHILOSOPHY OF CRITICISM

ON AMERICAN LIFE

ADAM, THE BABY, AND THE MAN FROM MARS

.·.

ON AMERICAN LEISURE

THE best test of the quality of a civilization is the quality of its leisure. Not what the citizens of a commonwealth do when they are obliged to do something by necessity, but what they do when they can do anything by choice, is the criterion of a people's life. One can tell much about a man by noting the objects and pastimes to which he spontaneously turns for joy. The same may be said of a nation. It was a suggestive comment of Maxim Gorky's on visiting Coney Island, 'What an unhappy people it must be that turns for happiness here.' The most serious criticism leveled against American civilization is not that its work is standardized and its business engulfing, but that its pleasures are mechanical and its leisure slavish. It is not that we have not time. Foreign observers are repeatedly as-

3

tonished at the number of hours an ever-increasing number of Americans have to themselves. It is not time that we lack, but leisure.

Leisure is indeed an affair of mood and atmosphere rather than simply of the clock. It is not a chronological occurrence but a spiritual state. It is unhurried pleasurable living among one's native enthusiasms. Leisure consists of those pauses in our lives when experience is a fusion of stimulation and repose. Genuine leisure yields at once a feeling of vividness and a sense of peace. It consists of moments so clear and pleasant in themselves that one might wish they were eternal.

For traveled Americans, at least, the best illustrations and memories of such experience will come from abroad. For one it will be the recollection of keen but casual conversation at tea on a lawn in Sussex or Surrey. For another it will be the image of two friends chatting over coffee and liquors at an *al fresco* table on a boulevard in Paris. Another will remember a stroll in an Italian piazza or the long, dignified peace of an evening in a London club.

It is not that one cannot find domestic images, too, of a quality of leisure that seems to be passing almost completely out of the

4

American scene. Many a middle-aged American, in the midst of a life crowded with social as well as business or professional obligations, will recall some rare hour that in its golden and gratuitous irrelevance seems to belong not in the realm of time but in the careless length of eternity, an afternoon spent browsing without purpose in a library or walking without the thought of time or destination on the quiet windings of an unfrequented country road. One recalls conversations lightly begun after dinner and meandering through wreaths of smoke into unexpected depths and intensities until long after an unnoticed midnight. One remembers some incredibly remote year when one wrote by hand a letter that flowed on as if ink and paper and ideas would never end.

But for Americans the word 'leisure' has distinctively Old World associations. That is partly because some Americans have there known it best. Cut off from the pressure and compulsions of their normal occupations at home, they have moved with freedom amid the grace of a leisurely tradition. But there is a deeper reason which lies in the contrast between that European tradition and our own. The quality of leisure in Europe is partly

5

the heritage of a long leisure-class tradition, partly the patience of peoples that have the sense of age and are not obsessed with hastening toward the new and building the possible in a hurry. In our own civilization, originally and in spirit partly pioneer, there is a working-rather than a leisure-class tradition, and the impress and atmosphere of work have come to control our lives even when we are not working. To be busy has been with us a primary virtue, and even our play has had to find a place for itself as a kind of business.

A number of years ago Professor Veblen in his 'Theory of the Leisure Class' tried to point out how the traditions and interests of a leisure class had shaped our tastes and our morals. A quite plausible volume might be written on the thesis that the pursuit of leisure in our civilization is determined by our traditions of work; we carry the morals and ideals of an essentially industrial, essentially business civilization over into our play. Leisure — a quiet and emancipated absorption in things and doings for their own sake — has always seemed to us effeminate and exotic. We wish leisure for relief, for release, for escape; for instruction, enlightenment, or advancement. There is something

6

immoral about moments that are good in themselves. There is probably no other country in the world where idleness is one of the deadly sins.

With us, therefore, leisure has been a melodramatic escape into excitement, or a moralistic flight into self-improvement. We oscillate between night clubs and outlines of culture. Every one has at some time or other been present at a determinedly gay party. He has seen ordinarily quiet, intelligent people become wilfully noisy and stupid. He has seen men and women, separately delightful and entertaining, prance about loudly, screaming vulgarities, acting the 'grown-up babies of the age.' And his pain has been increased by a sense that none of these people cared to do the silly things they were doing. They drank more than they really wished to, and uttered hiccoughing nonsense that they themselves despised.

Every one, likewise, has listened to a group of people at dinner or afterwards, talk with obligatory boredom about the modish books and plays and ideas. Spontaneity, which is of the essence of any truly spiritual life, flies out of the conversation and out of the window, when 'culture' becomes deliberate. We settle down as grimly to being serious as we settle down to being silly. Between the foolish and the funereal we have managed to find no middle course.

Of escapes from the pressure of an increasingly mechanized life to occasional outbursts of excitement or triviality there is much to be said. At least it may be said for them that they are natural, perhaps needful, refuges from a world whose tightly woven days would otherwise be unbearable. It is perhaps a sad commentary on the angular and constricted lives we lead that we should have to seek such lurid or futile ways to peace. But it is not to be wondered at that, living in such a world of routine, we should plunge ever so often into the loud nonsense of inane parties, wallow in the absurd pathos and comedy of the screen, or fall enraptured victims to successive crazes of footless puzzles and dull games. We may be forgiven our excursions to musical comedies without wit or music, and conversational evenings without humanity or ideas. The contemporary citizen is vexed beyond his own realization by the humdrum unthrilling pressure of his days; he craves naturally now and then an opportunity to be trivial, irresponsible, and absurd.

But the irony of our situation lies in the fact that even when we try to escape into triviality or foolishness we make a serious and standardized business of it. One can pardon occasional madness in a sober civilization, but there is something pathetic, almost ghastly, in soberly making madness a routine. The half-drunken gayety that has become the accompaniment of much respectable social life is a sad determined business. Orgy has become a social obligation; dissipation a prescription to the weary, the repressed, and the disenchanted. It becomes as much a social obligation to play a new game or have a new thrill as to read a new book or wear a current collar or hat. Any number of 'nice' people go systematically about becoming on occasion trivial, foolish, or mad. It is as if the American could not stop being efficient when he wanted to, and had to be gay or trivial or ecstatic with the same thoroughness and strained energy with which he might build a business or a skyscraper.

There are other reasons besides our own solemn efficiency that have been transforming our attempts to amuse ourselves into pale and

9

standard routines. The same forces that have gone into the big business of providing our necessities have gone into the big business of providing our amusements. One may glamorously state the possibilities of the radio, the universalization of beautiful music and distinguished thought. One may talk as one will about the possible high art of the moving picture, marvel as one will at the new mechanical perfections of the phonograph. There is no question but that these are at their best mechanical. They turn our leisure into a passive receptivity of standard mediocre amusement. They provide almost nothing of that spontaneous sense of individual living which is part of the repose and stimulation of leisure. It is not pleasant to realize that our leisure is taking on the color — or colorlessness — of the rest of our lives; that we are becoming stereotypes in our play as in our work. The most serious spiritual danger of the Industrial Revolution is that it has come to mechanize and industrialize not merely things but the spirit as well.

When a man is at leisure we like to say he is free to be himself, but if his freedom consists in efficiently amusing himself according to the standard formulas or subjecting himself to the passive reception of standard amusements, he is not free at all.

But while leisure has in one direction gone toward conventional amusement and stereotyped triviality, in another direction it has become a kind of elegant overtime work. The latest use we have found for leisure is to make it useful. Its usefulness, which might have been supposed to be that it was a good in itself, has been transformed into its possibility as a means of systematic self-improvement. Correspondence courses, outlines of knowledge, scrapbooks of learning — agencies not always disinterested — have been trying to teach us what we might do with our unharnessed moments if only we would harness them. A little less carousal and a little less bridge, and we might become heirs to all of Western culture, or experts in philosophy or French. There is a revealing irrelevance in the reasons assigned for turning the casual moments of our lives to the pursuit of knowledge. It is not that knowledge will render us self-possessed and whole, that it will give wings to our imagination and give a larger, clearer, and sweeter horizon to our lives. It is that knowledge, or a smattering of it, will make us successful or respected, that a veneer of garbled French will reveal our breeding, or a parade of the names of philosophers testify to our intellectual curiosity. There is possibly no clearer index to the remoteness of a native American culture than the eager indiscriminate voracity with which Americans gobble up tabloid versions of fields of expert knowledge. Far from meaning that we have turned to the love of wisdom, it means that we have turned our idle hours into the hurried business of getting short cuts to knowledge. Outlines simply are a way of applying efficiency to culture as well as to business. Their very essence is to say that here is all philosophy or history or literature for those who have not the patience or sympathy to explore any corner of any of them with disinterested delight. Worst of all, they have taken from leisure its saving essence — the sense of doing some lovely thing for its own lovable sake.

There are aristocratic pessimists in our midst who hold that leisure in the sense of a fine spontaneous use of free time is increasingly impossible in America. They point to the facts cited in the foregoing and to other equally distressing social habits. The omnipresence of the automobile is not simply a temptation to literal speed, but has come to be a symbol for speed in spiritual matters as well. The only excitement in any activity, even in the pursuit of truth, is the excitement of going fast. It is for that reason, they insist, that there is no country where ideas become popular so fast as in America, no country where, half-learned, they are so quickly outmoded and forgotten. A book is the book of a month or at most a season, and the rapid-transit reader comes to forswear books for the reviews of them, and forswear reviews for excerpts from them in a synthetic magazine.

It is pointed out again, and with justice, that the multiplication of physical luxuries and physical distractions is a constant intruder upon that collectedness of spirit in which alone leisure can come to being. Serenity and integrity are menaced as much by the telephone as by any single invention of the last century. Long quiet waves of time have become almost impossible in evenings shattered by radios, by movies, and by the constant seduction and noise of the automobile. Speculation begins in a dreaming fantasy; meditation in reverie. In our contemporary urban world one almost never has a chance to achieve that half-drowsy detachment in which fantasy and reverie begin. We are kept too wide-awake ever to be really at peace or in thought. Finally, in a country where there is still a glamorous sense of unlimited opportunity, the desire for first place makes almost impossible that freedom and detachment which leave one free to follow an impulse for its own self-rewarding delight.

The desire for speed, the desire for luxury, the desire for first place — these are indeed three deadly enemies of leisure. In the current movement of American life there is not much prospect of radically overcoming them. But there are portents of a change in our point of view that may portend a radical change in our practice.

There are growing evidences of a hunger for quiet and unhurried living among an increasing number of Americans. One cannot — nor would one — abolish the telephone or the automobile. There is no use in sighing for an anachronistic Paradise. It is impossible to transform life in New York in the twentieth century into the retirement of a rectory in Kent in the eighteenth. One cannot in the noise and hurry of a Western metropolitan winter pretend one

is living in the timeless unconcern of an East-
ern tropical island.

But part of our difficulty lies not in the im-
possibility of our circumstances, but in the
blindness of our philosophy. If we once learned
to rediscover the values of quiet spaces in our
lives we should find a way to find them. There
is time to be had even in New York or Chicago,
and solitude even among crowds. One need not
follow Thoreau into the wilderness to practice
his isolation, nor Buddha into the desert to
achieve his meditation. There is peace in a
city apartment if one will but stay at home an
evening to find it, and Nirvana to be found at
home in one's own mind.

Ultimately the lack of leisure is lack of spiritual integration. We flee to society, dull though
it be, through the fear of the greater dullness
of being alone. We hurtle along at a breakneck
speed, physically and spiritually, for fear of the
drabness and futility we might feel if we slowed
down. Any number of people are suddenly becoming aware of that situation and honest with
themselves; are beginning to realize how much
leisure one might have if one had enough faith
in one's own resources. One need not let life be
shattered into a splintered busyness by a rou-

tine absorption into social evenings which give one a standard good time. The rediscovery of solitude is being made by Americans, and with that rediscovery come many other delightful things: the chance to do nothing at all, not even talk, and the chance out of that interlude to follow a fancy or meditate a dream. Many a good citizen, given a chance to be alone with himself for an evening, might discover for the first time the quality of his own character, the contours of taste and interest that make him a personality as well as a jobholder and taxpayer. In such an interval a man may discover a hobby that will be for him a substitute for creative genius. He may not paint, write, or compose, but he may learn to do something indelibly himself and make something incredibly his own.

But in the golden days of leisure, in the spacious and graceful society of the Renaissance or the English country house, obviously men and women did not retire into their own souls away from the stimulation of other people. Good conversation is certainly one of the most enlivening ways of leisure, and good conversation is something between solemnity and absurdity. In America, of late, we have had to choose between talking on 'subjects' solemnly and schematically, or babbling nonsense, doing anything rather than talk. We are, I think, beginning to learn again the joy of conversation, a light and easy play of minds and tempers over common human themes. We have grown a little weary of talk that is all smart and burnished; we have grown tired, too, of talk that sounds like the overflow program of a literary club. We are learning again that the meeting of minds and moods is one of the sweetest and most amiable fruits of human society. It has its own novelties and excitements no less than the automobile, radio, and bridge.

Not but that these last have their own special value as the pure gold of leisure. Even the mania for speed has about it something of the quality of poetry. No one who on some moonlight night has sped along a country road will deny the sheer poetical appeal there is in the ease and freedom of speed. But the automobile has made the more peaceful kind of leisure possible as it never was before. It has brought the city dweller within easy reach of green and solitude. It has made neighbors of involuntary hermits. The radio, too, for all its

17

blare of tawdry music, has put millions within the reach of formerly impossible musical beauty. It has brought Beethoven to the farmer and to apartment dwellers who could never be lured to Carnegie Hall. And bridge, sniffed at by the cultured moralist, has its own justification. It is a diverting and harmless adventure of the mind and has for its devotees its own glories of wonder and conflict and surprise. If all these things are less interesting ultimately than conversation it is because we are social minds rather than aleatory machines.

There is, paradoxically enough, an incredible romanticism in our efficient impatience with leisure. We chase as madly as any early nineteenth-century German poet the Blue Flower of Happiness always beyond the hill. It is for that reason that we cannot take our idleness for the happiness it is; we try to turn it into an instrument toward the happiness it may bring. It may bring all knowledge into our province, or all salaries into our reach. It is for that reason that we have turned to outlines of knowledge and courses in success. But here, too, a change in spirit is notable.

There are men one knows who have made the surprised and delighted discovery that it is possible, if not to become hastily omniscient, at least to become patiently at home in some small field of knowledge or some tiny technic or art. It is not easy or particularly joyous to go into the whole vague history of mankind; but it is possible with pleasure to know one period or one decade of American history, or the story of one man or one movement. Only an octogenarian genius can master the whole of comparative literature; but any one can carve out a little pathway of poetry or prose, make one author, one genre, one theme his own, be it Trollope or sonnets, whaling or ballades. It is not possible for every man to be an artist; but almost any one can learn to draw or model, to play an instrument or plant a garden. In England one meets omniscient people no more than in America; nor are artists in every lane. But there are thousands of unpretentious lawyers or business men who have made some intimate little field of knowledge or thought their own, or learned to do one modest small hobby well.

We may talk much about the future of America, and think to measure its destiny by statistics of its educational, economic, or political changes. But the outlook for our country lies in the quality of its idleness almost as much as anything else.

Shall we then always alternate between trivial escapes into foolishness and solemn plunges into exploitation of our moments of repose? For us, as for Aristotle, there must be a golden mean. We may learn still to be at peace long enough to think and dream after our own fashion. We may learn to be together and be gay without being rowdy. We may learn to be expert in some little territory of art or thought or science without losing the amateur touch. We may still find time to live rather than time to kill.

If we do, we shall have learned what the spiritual life really means. For it means nothing more than those moments in experience when we have some free glint of life for its own sake, some lovely unforced glimmer of laughter or reason or love.

ON MEETING AMERICANS ABROAD

AND DISCOVERING ONE'S OWN COUNTRY THERE

It has become a commonplace that one of the best spots in which to study America in our time is Europe. That is not simply because of the obvious fact that American method and the American tempo are becoming omnipresent in the food, the dancing, and the business of European life. It is because of the still more obvious, almost irritating fact that one cannot any longer spend any length of time abroad without meeting one's fellow countrymen. It is no longer simply in summer or in Paris that you encounter them. You may find yourself in the heart of Touraine in February or at Nice in August, in the high obscure hill city of Gubbio or in some village tucked away in the wildest of North Wales; the familiar tone, profile, and gesture of a fellow-American are more than likely to appear. If you did nothing else for a year in Europe but study the Americans you met, you would have accomplished a year's important work in sociology.

In a year abroad spent on various parts of

the Continent one is sure to meet every variety of American, from the notorious loud-mouthed and quick-paced tourist to the expatriate dawdling out the decline of his life on the disdainful height of an olive-clad villa above the Arno. America abroad constitutes a country whose population is always more or less transient. Its philosophy, as various as the purse of its inhabitants, is controlled always in some measure by the fact that those inhabitants are away from home. If you are fatuously determined while in Europe to be a European, seeing Americans will be a constant source of irritation. It is hard, just when you feel that you have become *pro tem* a Frenchman or a Tuscan, to find yourself jolted back to Dayton or Detroit. But if you are frankly more or less preoccupied even when abroad with your own land, America in Europe becomes another continent to explore.

In a certain sense you discover your fellow countrymen for the first time when you meet them away from their usual haunts. Whether they have come for a month to see the whole Continent or have lived for a decade in one corner of it, what they have that is characteristically American stands out in almost brazen relief. You come to be aware, as never before, of the American voice when you hear it suddenly in the shrill staccato chatter of an Italian market-place. It may come as a jarring unmusical shock, this familiar drawling monotone, after the musical cadences of French or English speech. It may come as a fine homely suggestion of a hundred mingled memories of home. You may overhear a slang epithet that you have not heard in months, and it will recall forcibly the intense nervous definiteness of a civilization you thought for the time to have completely deserted. You may notice the tilt of a hat or the movement of a hand that in some unaccountable way spells America, or a touch of bright brassy humor that could be none other than transatlantic in its source.

Time and again you come upon America in a phrase, a joke, an intonation, or a gesture, and you are led to ruminate a little on your compatriots. What are they doing here, these energetic countrymen of ours who pass from Paris to Madrid, from Amsterdam to Berlin, as they might from Albany to Rochester. Why have they come? What are they getting out of it? What makes them so immediately and irretrievably different from these natives, among

23

whom they move so quickly and so hermetically, and from all other travelers in these foreign lands?

Perhaps it is the new cheap rates to Europe or that Europe has ceased to be merely a place to visit museums or to buy hats. But there are whole new classes of Americans you meet abroad who cannot be dismissed as conventional quick-trotting tourists or vulgar itinerant millionaires. Heaven and the irritated Continental know that there are still sufficient of these; more, doubtless, than ever. You know where to find and how to avoid them, these hurried idlers who make a loud summer resort of Paris and a loud winter resort of Nice. There is almost nothing in the way of atmosphere they could not find as well or as badly in Atlantic City or in the boom cities of Florida; wines, French dishes, and French shops are about the only differences that distinguish their lives abroad from the lives they would find at equivalent places at home. Almost they need not be studied at all in this connection, for in a consequential sense they are not in Europe.

But Europe is filled these days with a younger America that is here for good and

24

serious reasons and has an almost pathetic earnestness in getting something out of it. You meet young men and women in all parts of Europe staying for longer or shorter periods, and for more or less special purposes. An increasing number of fellowships for travel and study abroad pour each year upon the Continent a whole stream of youngsters in their twenties. It is not the conventional grand tour. For these travel stipends are, even with the present rate of exchange, not too large. Many of these post-collegians live and travel in Europe even more frugally than they would live and travel at home. They are to be found in the most modest of *pensions* or wandering in the most out-of-the-way towns and museums.

In Italy they are discoverable spending a month in Florence, trying to swallow *en même temps* the whole of Renaissance art, the whole of the Italian language, and all of Fascism. In Paris you will have to look for them far from the mundane crowd, in some *pension*, or in some family far from the rue de Rivoli, deeper by a good deal in Racine than in Montmartre. Nearly all of them have the haunting presentiment that they may never be in Europe again, and they are counting their minutes as well as their pennies. There is astonishing intensity and efficiency in their attempts to get all there is and all at once. They never miss doing or seeing the native and revealing things of the places at which they happen to be. They will be sure to hear the classics at the Comédie Française, and be present in Siena for the summer festa. In Southern France they will not miss the local wine or the local *entremets*. All over the Continent they will avoid English when they can, and in England they will try to speak it particularly well. There is none keener than they for detecting the unique qualities and characters of places visited, or reading themselves into sympathy with the objects of their pilgrimage. In their memories and in their collected mementoes they are storing up Europe for life.

The young student-wanderers have, of course, the weaknesses of all tourists. They like, for one thing, to feel that they have been where few others have ever gone. It is nice to come home having Ragusa and Helsingfors as well as Paris and London under your cap. They will occasionally be contemptuous of their own country in the enthusiasm of visiting another, or be impatient of a foreign land in the homesick memory of their own. For like other travelers they do grow homesick. Many a student ploughing through Dante in a room in a *pension* in Rome, or through Lamartine in a room in a *pension* in Paris, lives spiritually half the time in his letters to and from home. With all the help afforded by the university unions and the international committees, the student abroad, or the student-traveler abroad, very seldom penetrates into the intimate domestic life of the country in which he happens to be. One out of twenty comes home having acquired a European friend. Few of them in a year come to know familiarly a European family. Very few of them certainly feel themselves Europeanized at the end of a year, and almost none wishes to become expatriate. Long before the end of the year their eyes and imaginations are turned with childlike eagerness toward home.

Where they do get to know or get to be known by Europeans, they are among our best ambassadors. They do much to disabuse the European of the notion that every American is a millionaire. They help to clear them of the belief that most of us are vulgarians. To meet them abroad is to have a sudden pride and a kindled hope in the possibilities of American youth. It is to have a sudden sense also of the distinctive character of that youth, and of its special limitations and indubitable special virtues. They are a well set-up lot, these American student-travelers, for one thing, and display a certain fresh antiseptic energy that marks them out when they appear among a group of Continental students. The American student of, say, twenty-three seems ridiculously naïve compared with some of the eighteen-year-old students among whom he studies when he settles down for a while at a Continental university. He still has to find out the elements of subjects and ideas whose complexities they have long ago taken for granted. His Continental acquaintances are often amused by both his intellectual and moral innocence. The English student's conversation will be sprinkled with casual references to the classics of his own and of ancient tongues; the German student will mingle politics with metaphysics; the Italian student will move easily in the history of fine art and in the ways of the world. All this will bewilder and discourage the American fresh from his B.A. For the wandering bachelor of arts is innocent morally as well as intellectually. A meeting with young Americans abroad sometimes prompts you to consider what babes may win degrees, and degrees with honor, from an American university.

But most of them, at least in the experience of the writer, do not try to hide or belittle their naïveté. Some of them, away for the first time from the restraints of their usual environment, are in terrific haste to remedy their state of innocence. They ape a culture they do not yet possess and a deviltry they do not care for. But you are struck peculiarly by their balance, their eagerness, and their good sense. They live in Europe usually as discriminating Americans, not as the æsthete's imitation European. They get Europe without succumbing to it. Their six months or a year abroad does not disenchant them with America. It gives them a perspective on it; it helps them to live more fully as citizens of their own country, and as citizens of the world in whose fortunes that country is involved.

It is hard to speak as highly of the summer migration of undergraduates. For them the new cheap ocean rates have made possible a quick lurid holiday in Europe. Many an innkeeper on the Continent has mixed memories of American collegian visitors. You wonder whether the average American collegian on his return has clear memories of anything. But for even the most scatter-brained of them Europe must be at least a visual experience. For those with any degree of intelligence or feeling, even a hurried trip through the Continent or England must make literature and history much less a matter of hearsay when they return in the autumn. The sound of French or the look of Oxford must be for many of them an elementary lesson in cosmopolitanism.

There are other Americans you meet in Europe whose presence you cannot so clearly account for. In many cases you are certain that Europe is for them in the nature of some sort of flight from boredom, from perplexity, from disappointment. If you meet such cases in a lonely place, a little off the beaten track, where America seems very far away, you may, over a bottle of wine, learn why they are there.

The writer has met in the course of less than a year at least a dozen men between the ages of twenty-five and thirty-five who have discovered at the end of several years in some business or profession that they did not like it. They have come to spend their accumulated savings and an uncertain length of time to try to think out what they should do next. They drift through Europe from one place to another, not much caring where, until their minds are made up or their purses exhausted. For them the charm of the Continent consists chiefly in the fact that it is three thousand miles from home, and that they are for a time where they are known by nobody and where they owe explanations to no relatives. Or you run into men who persist in believing that they can come to Europe and leave their crucifixion of spirit at home.

There are older people, elderly married couples, released by a small funded income to wander aimlessly and not very happily from one famous place to another. They do not know when or if they are ever coming home, or why they are staying, or quite why they came. They are pathetic castaways living aimlessly in no world at all. There are sad-eyed men and women of varying ages who have come to forget something or other, and in the loneliness of distance they will tell you, perhaps, what they have come to forget or how lonely they are.

Even people you think to have known fairly well at home will in the stimulation and liberation of being in a foreign country suddenly reveal themselves as they would not dream of doing or dare to do in twenty years' conversation at home. There are professors who will betray their disillusion with scholarship or education, or who will lapse into sentiment or sentimentalism that they would never permit themselves amid the respectable frigidities of a campus. There are business men who have a surprising childishness and humility here amid the inconveniences of a foreign language and far from their telephones and secretaries. All their brusque efficiency is gone, and in Sicily or at Cap d'Antibes they may suddenly confess a doubt about the distant busy preoccupations of their lives.

Some of the driftwoods seem bound to stay forever, if they have any income and if they consider the rate of exchange. It is certainly the low rate of exchange in the Latin countries that is responsible for the large semi-permanent literary colony you meet nowadays abroad. Nor is this literary colony simply a long-talking non-working Bohemia. Paris and all of Italy are filled with industrious literary men who

32

find it convenient to live where American checks will pay for taxis instead of subway tickets, and where the receipts of one fairly successful book will permit life in semi-luxury for a year. These also can hardly be described as really living abroad. For what is alive in them, their spirit, is at home. Their intellectual food consists largely of American books, periodicals, and press-clippings. Their social life consists largely in conversation with kindred Americans settled like themselves for reasons of convenience in Europe.

But it is not the low exchange that explains the presence of the large body of expatriates you meet all over Europe, especially in Paris and Italy. These permanent exiles are a sadly interesting lot. They are interesting if for no other reason than that they remain sometimes after twenty years inescapably American. They betray themselves to the visitor from home by their wistful, half-concealed, half-feverish concern with events and personalities in the land they have deserted. They are Rip Van Winkles who have been all these years only half asleep, and in their dozing have caught whispers of the world to which they were once awake. They seem, many of them, to be minor characters out of the less compe-tent of Henry James's novels. You are pecul-iarly sure to find them in or above Florence, among the hills of the island paradise of Capri, among the almost luridly lyrical colors of Ta-ormina. For it is Europe as a soft æsthetic refuge that has brought and kept these here. A rococo villa above the Arno is their surrogate for the Ivory Tower. Twenty years in Italy have made them not the least Italian in their tastes or sympathies. Their Italian is often primitive, and they know no natives other than their servants or Andrea del Sarto and Botticelli. Theirs is a closed world consisting of luncheon parties at each other's villas, or the entertainment, sometimes on a grand scale, of a tolerable spirit from the barbarous active frontier world which they disdain from afar. A faint scorn and a faint unmistakable discon-tent are in their voices, their faces, and their words. They will never come home, and, for all their obvious luxury and apparent peace, they have for twenty years been spiritually starved and emotionally homeless. They have lost contact with the only public opinion that has any meaning for them. There is nothing particularly exciting to do, and the rôle of spectator has lost all its excitements, since the spectacle is no longer a novelty. They are the most unhappy Americans in Europe. They are homesick, and they will never come home.

Out of these multitudinous impressions of these so various Americans you meet abroad, you begin to frame an impression of a civilization whose *mores* have combined to stamp a race. The theory of the melting-pot may be true or false; the anthropologists may argue that out among themselves. The notion of an American race may be a fairy-tale or a remote possibility. But meeting your fellow countrymen abroad leads you to accept the fairy-tale and believe in the possibility. It is more than the lean jaw, the straight head, the even, always slightly nasal voice. They may be young or old, eager tourists or disillusioned exiles; they have certain common qualities that are as striking as the dark skin of the Italians or the reticent unconcern of the Britisher. The very qualities that sometimes make them offensive in Europe are the defects of a certain rough virtue.

Mark Twain long ago celebrated with broad strokes and defensive sympathy the American innocent abroad. He made most persuasive that honest provincialism which refuses to

think of guides as prophets or of guide-books
as Bibles, and which will not be bulldozed into
awe by things that are simply famous or old.
One has laughed a thousand times over Americans who divide among themselves the task of
seeing a museum, or let one member of a family
do the outside of a cathedral while the other
one takes the inside. But there is something to
be said for the traveler who will not stay more
than ten minutes in the Pitti Palace in Florence
if he finds the pictures dull. Much of what is
condemned as Philistinism may be defended as
honesty; much that passes for crudeness is
simply lack of cultural pretense.

The American, especially the young American abroad, is often sniffed at for too much
humility rather than for too little. There is of
course, Mark Twain's impudent rough-neck
who blows out a light that he learns has been
burning a thousand years. But there are thousands of others all too ready to think that any
little light of other days outshines even the
blazing contemporary sun. There are number-
less youths too timid to be outright American,
and anxious to be courteously imitative of
other people's habits and manners and accents.
But if a youngster is humble for a time in

Europe, it will not hurt him or hurt his capacity to be a citizen of his own time and country. Why should he not be hushed into humility by a civilization whose mere age and range must bewilder a young citizen of a young country? When he gets home there will be plenty of people about, to teach him respect for the bright and shining and new.

'Punch' smiled once at a mythical American girl who asked a London policeman the nearest way to an English skylark. But that naïve hunt for background was based, after all, on a loving acquaintance with Shelley. There is, after all, something appealing in a traveler who goes hunting for a skylark of which a poet has caused her to dream.

The roughness and the humility, the nervous haste, the nostalgia and the sense of alienation that are revealed by Americans in Europe are symptoms of the fact that the American abroad is a type and a character. He is always a stranger, a rather self-conscious stranger in a world he feels to be different from his own. It is from that sense of difference often that an American learns to discover his own country, and his own implication in its life and fortunes. He goes home, in most cases, a rather finer

American. Europe has become naturalized in his eyes and imagination; often for the first time America has become naturalized in his head and heart.

AMERICAN CHARACTER AND
COLLEGE EDUCATION

A CONSIDERATION of the original function of the American college throws considerable light on what is still to-day its peculiar, privileged — and neglected — business. The original New England colleges were founded primarily to train ministers, the accredited shepherds of character in colonial days and in the early days of the Republic.

Those student ancestors of ours were expected to emerge disciplined spirits, as well as informed minds. The theological intention, the clerical atmosphere, have gradually if incompletely faded from collegiate halls. But there has remained among literate Americans the sense that there is a moral justification for the four years of late adolescence that a boy or girl spends at college. The American faith in college education has rested in no small measure on the assumption that a college education, like a religion seriously believed in or a philosophy seriously accepted, makes a difference in the 'way of life.' Nobody has ever honestly contended that four years could turn a high-

school graduate into a scholar. But generations of American parents have believed that
four years at college would make a difference
in that complex amalgam of manners, controlling ideas, and habitual emotions that go to
make up what we call 'character.' It has been
vaguely but pertinaciously felt that for good
or ill the college does make a moral difference, a
subtle and pervasive change in the way a youth
will lead his life.

One hesitates a little to use the expression
'moral influence' at all. The word 'moral' has
certainly come into disrepute among the sophisticated. It connotes too much pietistic
unction and traditional fraud. Neither the
parents of college students nor college students
themselves wish in the old sense to be Made
Good or to be taught to Be or Do Good. And
the colleges, many of them merely feeders to
the professional schools of the universities,
many of them glorified trade schools, are quite
content to let problems of character and morals in the old sense go unregarded. But college students unwillingly find their characters
affected by their being at college; willy-nilly
the colleges exert a moral influence upon their
lives.

The colleges indeed affect character often where they are as institutions least conscious of doing so. They may do it primarily through setting a certain tone or manner which may be nothing more than an accent or a lifelong habit of nonchalance or disdain. There are colleges that by the sheer quietude and beauty of their surroundings leave an intimate and permanent impress, a *memoria sacra* that becomes a calm retrospective refuge for students in the later chaos of their lives. There are institutions, like some of the universities in the Middle West, where playing the game and with the gang become the civic habits of a lifetime. The influence of place or of tradition cannot be willed. In these respects, and quite advisedly, the colleges trust to luck concerning the influence they exert on their students. You cannot legislate a background or a *milieu* into being, as colleges that have tried it have learned to their blundering cost.

A second incidental but important way in which colleges affect the formation of character is through the obvious presence of character and characters on their faculties. It is often forgotten that teaching is communication by contagion and in the 'mystical contact of the classroom' a student often learns more from his professor than the subject that professor teaches. He imbibes a temper of life, an approach to all being that outruns the confines of any subject, and is more nicely effective than any express ethical teaching. This moral contagion is deeply accented by the fact that when a professor impresses the imagination of students at all, he has a chance to impress them more than many more distinguished adults whom the students later may meet. He is likely to be among the first persons of any distinction at all with whom the undergraduate has come in contact. Almost nobody can define what constitutes a good teacher, but every college possesses them and students are quick and certain to detect them. From them students carry away a certain spiritual essence; their intellectual habits and personal qualities are powerful suggestions of definitive ways of life to students whose imaginations are still more impressible than their reason.

There is, of course, a third and more deliberate way in which the colleges have from their foundation sought to affect and control the direction of their students' characters. I do not refer to police regulations of student leisure except for flagrant violations of decency or order. That is almost passing away. But the colleges have persisted in the assumption that theory does affect practice, and that deliberate courses in ethics will modify conduct. It would be hard to *under*estimate the net result of these courses. The late Stuart Sherman remarked that one of the troubles with college was that ethical instruction was left to elderly professors lecturing upon Aristotle, while the undergraduate's actual image of the Good Life came from his companions and from novels by authors in their undisciplined twenties. The first leaves them cold and the second leaves them agitated and blind.

The regulation college course in ethics is ineffective for a reason that Aristotle pointed out in his own 'Ethics' two thousand years ago. It is not theory but habit that governs human conduct, and no amount of study of the admirable moral ideas of Immanuel Kant or John Stuart Mill will solve the human conflicts or integrate the adolescent chaos of the undergraduate soul. There is, moreover, a special reason — which Aristotle could not have known about — why courses in ethics are of such nugatory consequence in the formation or

43

reformation of undergraduate character. They are taught generally by professors who happen to be more interested in the theory of Aristotle than in the living issues which confront their students. Such teachers are as effective as preachers would be who met the spiritual needs of their parishioners by acute analysis of the dialectical difficulties involved in transubstantiation.

The two deliberate methods — policing and lecturing — which colleges have used to reorganize the souls of their students have failed. But college administrators, and teachers interested in their students no less than in their subjects, have felt that the moral problems of students are still a chief business of the college, though there has been considerable change of opinion as to what those problems are or what their possible treatment should be. These problems are clearly its chief business because in a broad sense, they are the students' chief preoccupation during their college years, at least of that portion of the student body who have any reason to be at college at all. Often in lecturing to undergraduates on some theory of Spinoza or of Kant, one wonders what is passing through the heads of students, what, when they are thinking, these students think about. Occasionally in a conference concerning an essay or a bibliography, what they are thinking about will appear. It is not Spinoza or Kant. It is the problem of finding some integration, some moral resolution in a world of inner confusion. It is to find out what one is or what one ought to be.

There are certain arresting facts that urge these matters to the attention of both college teachers and college executives. A student may be failing in a course; a half hour's conversation sometimes brings to light the fact that he is failing for reasons that have little to do with the course and much to do with himself. A nervous breakdown, a sudden erratic withdrawal from college, or the ghastly melodrama of a suicide sometimes force those in collegiate authority to recognize that here in extreme form are elements of unrest and unhappiness that in less urgent guise are facing most students.

Now if it is the business of a college to do anything at all, that business certainly includes the function of enabling students before they have quit its precincts to find some peace in their own souls and some steadying adjustment to their world. Peace, for Spinoza, was through understanding, a complete and deliberate integration of one's own nature of things. The colleges can have no more vital function than the fostering of such an integration among students who in the privacy of an instructor's study or a chum's room will confess how agonizingly deep in disorder they are. It is very rare on a campus to find genuinely vicious or depraved characters. But it is equally rare to find character at all, in that definitive sense in which one speaks of the character of a writer or composer, character in the sense of a definitive direction, a personality with a center, edge, sturdiness, and depth. And one may say indeed that in so far as the colleges have succeeded in enabling students to approach a unification and clarification of themselves, in so far, in a word, as they have enabled them to achieve a character, they have performed the chief of their functions. As long as they proceed on the assumption that they are dealing with disembodied intelligence, separately measurable by tests, and not the complete and perturbed psyche of groping and disordered youth, they will be machines of instruction rather than centers of education. It is pathetic to observe

46

undergraduates going four years through college without having, so far as the college is concerned, received any help whatsoever in understanding those conflicts and disorders which render them so often lost souls and irrevocably. It is pathetic to observe and stupid to condone or continue.

There are, it appears to the writer, three directions in which the colleges may come to be more genuinely effective in making students at home with themselves and with their world. The first of these is a clearer understanding, a required clearer understanding, on the part of college teachers and administrators of the nature of those issues and conflicts which disintegrate so many undergraduates. The second is the presence on a college campus of a trained psychiatrist to whom cases of genuine nervous or psychical disintegration could be referred. The third is the provision of lecture and seminar courses in morals which will come to grips with the human issues that actually are moral issues to students, instead of treating them to and with the traditional casuistry of academic moralists.

First, as to the understanding of those elements which properly controlled go to make,

47

undisciplined go to destroy, any unification of personality among students. In the better secondary schools there is infinitely more understanding of contemporary psychological and psychiatric knowledge than is found among any but the smallest proportion of college instructors. The reason for this is to be found in the fact that in secondary schools, it is realized that the chief business of a teacher is teaching. In the colleges, especially in those that form parts of universities, the exact status of a professor is never clear. He is supposed to be a scholar who incidentally earns his salary by giving collegiate instruction. It does not matter that most of his time is taken up with the duties of teaching, nor that his primary gifts are in that direction, nor that he has a genuine interest in his students. It does not matter, on the other hand, if he has no gifts for teaching at all, if he begrudges the time it takes from his studies as time given to 'pushing the perambulator.' Both those who are fit material for college teaching and those who simply endure it and whom the students simply endure, are all engaged in dealing with undergraduates. A comparatively small number of the members of most college faculties know or care what their students are thinking about or troubled about, or how they 'get that way.' Those who do care, the 'professional fathers' weep and wish with the troubled boys rather than understand them.

William James coined the phrase, 'the sick soul.' Disordered soul would be a better name for that undergraduate psychic chaos which it is the business of college deans and teachers to understand. The disorder arises from several disillusions and detachments which the student suffers upon coming to college. One emotional snag which often comes to light in a student's personal problems is his family. For the first time physically and psychologically distant from it at college, he either has all the childhood standards removed, or he is haunted by them. He is either busy rebelling against or busy being obsessed by his family, and by his childhood moral fixations. The result is a complex agony of spirit which accounts for a thousand uneasinesses and restlessnesses in the life of the undergraduate. He is trying to become a self-sustaining adult in place of a psychically dependent child. He is trying to substitute standards of his own, which he has not yet found, for those imposed upon by the milieu

49

of the home. With the passing for him of the familiar childish morality which he no longer accepts, goes often and simultaneously the passing of religious sanctions (for all practical purposes associated with the training and traditions of his home). Nor is this all. At the same time that he is being released from those moral criteria with which he has come to college, he is undergoing two awakenings, one sexual, the other intellectual. Without too much exaggeration one may say that the former is the basis of his romantic idealisms, the latter of his skepticisms and despairs. It is sex in its reverberant forms that opens to him the whole rhapsodic landscape of love and rapture, of mysticism and poetry, confused as these are by physical promptings which he at once cherishes and distrusts. It is his intellectual awakening that is responsible for all that tumult of futilitarian cynicism and despair that inform and inflate so much of undergraduate poetry and conversation. It is his intellectual awakening that leads him to depression, to irritation, or to tortured parade of unconcern. The dawning of mind in the undergraduate is indeed better revealed and attested in him in the way he thinks about these personal problems than in the way he deals with courses where his memory and his routine habits of work are generally at a greater premium than his intelligence.

The awakened intelligence of the undergraduate is led to depression for several characteristic reasons. It is at college that he first becomes acutely aware of the discrepancy between things as he has perhaps roseately been taught to believe them, and things as he finds them to be. His adolescent thinking comes in conflict with his adolescent emotions. Just as the conditions of his own nature prompt his young spirit to their most romantic flights of idealism, his tyro intelligence becomes aware of how wide of the facts his dreams are. He is led to irritation at the stupidity of adults who will not order the world after the congenial canons of reason. His tortured paradise of unconcern is the flourish of an idealism a little self-conscious about baring its ideals or its frustrations to an unfeeling and a misunderstanding society.

His skepticisms, too, are the fruits of his awakened critical faculties, and they are concerned with three things: with himself, the nature of things, and the nature of that social world in which he finds himself. It is a commonplace to speak of the cockiness of adolescence. Where it is present, and it is present a great deal less than is commonly supposed, it is often too obviously the loud façade of shyness. But often even this façade is lacking, and there is revealed an almost flayed sensitiveness and humility. The undergraduate distrusts himself often directly as a result of one of the things that college has taught him, the touchstone of excellence from which he feels himself far. He is skeptical of the world of nature. Brought up as he probably is in the warm bath of belief in a providing Providence, he meets the cold shower of modern intellectualistic mechanism. The light goes out in Heaven and purpose out of the earth.

There are two outstanding explanations of why he comes to distrust the world of man. One is the shocked recognition of the difference between moral pretension and moral fact in society. The other is his awareness of the shoddiness of that commercial and social and even of much of that educational world into which he has entered. There is something more to be added to all these distrusts, irritation and depressions. There are the repressions which

come from habits and traditions from which
the undergraduate has not succeeded in freeing
himself. They are responsible for the innocent
things he refrains from doing and the cheap
things that out of braggadocio he does. All
these make for disintegration that in extreme
form leads to nervous breakdown or suicide.
In milder manifestations they comprise the
stock troubles of undergraduates. To paraphrase Matthew Arnold:

> Weary of himself and sick of asking,
> What he is or what he ought to be,

the undergraduate is not altogether inarticu-
late on either of the subjects. But there is an
intense discrepancy about the things he finds
himself thinking about and the things he is
expected to think about. Often he looks about
for aid, and he would at times accept it from
any one. Sometimes he finds a little of it
among sympathetic instructors, though their
help consists not seldom merely in uniformed
sentimentals, kindly condolences and cheery
prophecies that when the boy is as old as his
instructor he will get over it. Any college instructor whose personality is not positively
repulsive can recall dozens of these bruised
psyches that have crossed his path.

Colleges that try to do anything more than train discarnate minds must well consider the possibility of communicating some order to the distracted spirits of those who come to their doors. For out of these chaoses order may be made, out of this ferment a clear wine of life. There are chaoses that have gone too far for retrieval except under medical care. It is for these that the second recommendation was made, that of a trained psychiatrist for every college. It is not merely that these may avert an occasional suicide, but that they may help to remove psychic cancers that would otherwise render the lives of certain students lifelong paralysis.

But there are disorders that have not gone so far, and require only the understanding of students by themselves. For the former it is requisite that any one who goes into college teaching be at least minimally informed as to current psychological and psychiatric knowledge. And it is important, as William James long ago reminded college administrators, that college teachers be appointed, among other things, on the basis of their fitness to teach, as well as on the basis of their alleged competence in a subject. No amount of technical psychological knowledge or knowledge of any green field will compensate for a lack of those elementary virtues: tact, persuasive clarity, and an interest in students as human beings that are among the distinguishing marks of a good teacher.

For the understanding of students by themselves, many things remain to be done that can, I think, be done with some hope of success. Among the chief of these is a new type of course in morals which would probably have to be elective if it were to be of any use. Such a course, as I envisage it, would dispense almost completely with a study of traditional academic distinctions in ethics. It would deal directly and frankly with the kind of conflicts and issues which genuinely preoccupy the college boy or girl. It would resemble the case method in the law schools where a study of principles arises from a consideration of actual legal instances. The first effect of such a course — and it had better be a seminar or a conference rather than a course of lectures — should be to destroy in a student the feeling that the problems with which he was concerned were unique, isolated, and secret matters. Problems that had appeared to him feverishly individual would be discovered to be widespread; what had become a private hysteria would achieve the coolness of objective recognition. When problems of family, of sex, of religion, were displayed in their relation to the actual ways in which they confront students, the whole of the academic curriculum would cease to be severed from life. From the nightmare of personal difficulties the student would learn to enter the daylight of the open world. One of the most exquisite pains of adolescence is the desolate feeling that this so devastating unhappiness or uncertainty is a monstrous personal disaster, a strange unprecedented soliloquy. A course in morals that dealt with these difficulties common to ninety-nine out of a hundred students would do much to give the student the peace of perspective and the integration that comes from understanding the status of one's own difficulties in the light of the common plight and prospects of men.

The effect of such an enterprise would, it appears to me, work two ways. It would clear up those personal tangles which cloud and obstruct a student's encounters with his studies. On the other hand, those studies would themselves become meaningful as they impinged upon his clearer and freer mind. Religion, economics, philosophy would cease to be so many subjects. They would be appreciated as phases and aspects of that released and emancipated, disciplined and integrated individuality which is the aim ultimately of all education. Students might under some such régime become not simply bachelors of arts, but masters of themselves, clear and untroubled participators in the common adventure of mankind. They would cease to brood vacillatingly on inner tumults and come to look with candor and curiosity on the engaging possibilities of things. It is an experiment worth trying.

CAN AN ARTIST LIVE IN AN AMERICAN UNIVERSITY?[1]

FOR many reasons, most of them economic, writers in America live usually in a professional environment and among professional groups whose interests are far from being those of the literary artist. They are newspapermen; they are editors; they are teachers; they are advertising men; they are scouts for publishing houses or publicity agents for opera stars. Unless, of course, they are by chance richlings or by choice vagabonds. Few novelists and fewer poets can hope to make a living out of writing precisely and only the things they care as artists to write. As a consequence the most serious part of a writer's life and the deepest preoccupations of his spirit are often crowded into intervals stolen from the chief and public business of his days.

Many writers have tried and are trying to live in a university. For it must be remembered that when a man starts to teach he does

[1] This essay appeared as one of a series called "Can an Artist Live in America?"

not simply spend a few hours a day on a campus discussing Keats or Plato with sophomores and sophomores with his colleagues. He finds himself within a year or two living in as special, absorbing, and, in some ways, as corruptive a society (corruptive to his interests as a writer) as it would be possible to find in America.

The reasons why a man with the soul, the instincts, the equipment, and the ambitions of a writer often settles down to a university career are obvious and familiar. Toward the end of his college days an undergraduate who has written verse and prose for the campus papers discovers in himself the definite conviction that he must be a writer. The profession of college teaching offers a modest income and a relatively large amount of leisure. Surely if it has been fun to read Keats and Swinburne and Shaw it will be fun to talk about them to agreeable young men. And certainly there is no other job in the offing that promises freedom every week-end and all summer. Many a novelist and many a poet has been seduced into teaching by a consideration of those periods in a teacher's life when he is not teaching at all.

It is not simply the free time but the apparent freedom of spirit that attracts the young artist. The university looks to him like a humane monastic citadel peopled by choice citizens with interests more stirring and lovely than those meaner concerns one would run into in 'the great outside world.' Here at least is a retreat in the midst of American life where there is no competition for non-essentials, no bartering of one's æsthetic or moral integrity for luxury or first place. The prizes are limited and they are measurably secure. If one cannot live at the Ritz all winter — and why would one want to? — one can bicycle and dream through Wessex all summer. If one is not forever in the hum of affairs one will move daily in the center of ideas. One will be able to watch and report, without being overwhelmed, the loudness, the vulgarity, the haste of the market-place. A sensitive college senior judges the academic atmosphere largely from those finer-tempered undergraduates who have been his friends and whom he knows infinitely better than he knows the faculty. He may well suppose that nowhere would one find more food for thought or more incitement to the expression of subtle feeling than in the intercourse of a group of scholars dining together on a high academic hill.

The young artist may feel, too, that if he is going to be a writer he will have to write about something. It has doubtless occurred to him that it is not the ignorant or the instinctive who have written the commanding books of the world. Milton's scholarship, he notes, does not seem to have hurt but seems rather to have deepened and solidified his poetry. The 'Paradiso' of Dante would doubtless not have culminated in such sheer concluding rapture if it had not risen from the discipline and depths of profound acquaintance with Plato and Aquinas. The undergraduate writer has read — and remembered — 'The Scholar Gipsy,' nor have any of the bright moderns altogether cured him of his love for Matthew Arnold. He settles down, then, with a splendid and naïve intention to be a scholar poet, or, like Zona Gale (who is a trustee of a university) or like May Sinclair (who is a metaphysician), a novelist with a mind, a background, and a philosophy.

In several respects he is spinning lovely contraries to fact. The leisure he has anticipated is, like many other soft illusions about life in the

61

academy, a myth. Academic leisure, he finds, is purely academic. If, as is not unlikely, he teaches the English he hoped some day to learn to write he will find his days spent in conference with students in matters of punctuation and syntax, and evenings that were to go to the writing of fiction will be devoted too often to the reading of themes. He will be forced to take over extension courses to help meet current expenses and summer-school teaching to pay for a trip abroad in some remote future summer. What leisure time he has during the year will go to grinding out a Ph.D. dissertation on a theme worthy the attention of a worm rather than a poet.

But even after he is safely ensconced in the comfortable rank of an assistant professor he will find, unless he is extremely self-possessed, that the university has got under his skin. He had imagined himself joining a society of free spirits moving in the communion of high, clear thoughts upon vivid perennial issues. Instead he finds himself caught in the treadmill of men who have the habits of mind of rather superior civil servants or the secular analogues of army officers at dull posts on remote frontiers. These men wear caps and gowns instead of uniforms;

they are preoccupied with literature or economics instead of printing or engraving or
ammunition. But like civil servants or army
officers they are absorbed in petty politics —
rumors of promotions, displacements, and
advancements — such as a mind engaged in
creation can only at its peril afford to bother
with at all. He will find that the whole pursuit
of writing is in most universities regarded not
as an art but as a low journalistic business.
One note in a philosophical journal, one textbook, one syllabus even will bring him more
respect among many of his colleagues and
certainly among his administrative superiors
than a poem, a short story, or a novel. Two
fears will obsess the young writer on a campus:
the fear of being thought facile by his colleagues
and the fear of being thought dull by his public. The net result is that he often succeeds
merely in being both. He writes too timidly
and too much.

It is the academic community with which he
daily comes in contact from which it will be
harder and harder in fact or in imagination to
escape. How is one after hours to stop being
the professor, especially if the college or university happens to be in a small town? Not

only the students who tip their hats to him on the campus but the townspeople too set him superstitiously apart. In a large city he can escape more easily. In ten minutes by subway or bus he can be where both he and his rank are unknown, or, if known, unimpressive. But even there he will not be able to erase the stamp of the university from his soul. It is not simply the worst features of campus of which he will have to beware: the committee meetings, the pedagogical shop-talk, the hierarchical gossip. The best things will be almost as fatal to him as an artist.

The life that he will come to love best as a teacher, for example, will hurt him indubitably as a writer. If a man is at all generous-minded he will not be able to resist giving the best that is in him to a body of young men who are, all things considered, as warm-hearted and intelligent a student class as one is likely to meet anywhere in the world. He will not dare to give a casual or slipshod lecture to a group containing at least one or two minds who, save in respect to the number of days already spent on earth, can hardly be rated as inferior to his own. To conduct a class of superior undergraduates for an hour is no slightly fatiguing matter. The man who tries to achieve beauty on paper will be no less solicitous of his performance in the classroom. But he can be a good teacher only at the expense of being a tired writer. And the qualities that will make him a good teacher, the ability to make things clear and vivid — to adolescents — will help to make him the author of an amiable textbook but hardly of a work of art.

In its noblest signification, it may be protested, a university is a society of inquiring scholars, not a regiment of pedagogues. To this it may be answered that that is what a university may be in essence, but not in American fact. Yet even the interests of a scholar, especially a scholar in an American university, may be perilous to a writer. Certainly literary and philosophical scholarship are largely retrospective. And however wide the business of scholars may sound, it is in fact minute and textual. Certainly, whatever else art may be, it is spontaneous and adventurous. It is the unpredictable use of fresh experience or experience freshly conceived. That is hardly the atmosphere in which American scholarship lives. The search for truth in our universities is frequently the search for commas. And it is conducted in an organization as hierarchical as that of the church, and quite as traditional.

The most characteristic aspect of a university, its intellectuality, or rather its intellectualism, can do an artist no good. A writer should have ideas surely. But ideas are really such only when they are sparks shot up by experience. They should not constitute the only experience a man has. At a university one moves among colleagues whose whole lives consist in ideas, and oftener still in the words which in the youth of their speakers stood for ideas. The writer on a campus finds himself moving in a systematized, a catalogued, what William James called a classroom universe. By thirty-five the professor-writer has become incorrigibly the professor. The caution of scholarship has become in him the timid fixity of the conservative. The dignity of the classroom has become his habitual all-day manner. His world has narrowed to 'a professor's house.' He may at best become a respectable critic. Journalism may seduce him from the campus, although he will always remain of it. But ten years in a university will kill the poet, the dramatist, the novelist he may have become. Longfellow and Lowell are sufficiently striking examples. If it

66

were not too unkind one could name half a dozen contemporary examples of writers of indubitable gifts whom habituation to a campus has killed.

For myself, small examples serving as well as large ones, I like the academic atmosphere. For mildly philosophical prose and minor reflective poetry it is as good a retreat as any. If I wanted to be a novelist I should flee it, though there is at least one good novel in every campus community. (Perhaps after writing it one would wish or have to flee.) As it is I am content. Even here in the glamor of the *quattrocento* at Florence I am homesick to talk to sophomores of Santayana. For in the long run I care almost as much about teaching and scholarship as I do about writing. That is one of the troubles with a university. That is one of the pleasant perilous things it does to a writer who lives within the walls too long.

JOHN DEWEY, AMERICAN

THE influence of John Dewey on American thought and education has been one of the notable, as it has been in some ways one of the mysterious features of American culture in the last thirty years. It has been notable because every liberal and releasing movement in philosophy, social reform and education has found in him a central and articulate voice. It has been mysterious because, for all his wide reputation, he is not widely read, and in many quarters where his name and authority are cited, he is not understood. Not one of his books has become a vogue after the fashion in which James Harvey Robinson's 'Mind in the Making,' and H. G. Wells's 'The Outline of History' had their hectic season of public recognition. There has never been any attempt on Professor Dewey's part to mitigate the difficulties of his generous but abstract thinking, to vivify or simplify his candid but complex style. If Dewey has become one of the major prophets of his day, it is certainly not because he has the seductive literary qualities of Santayana or the sensational and obvious novelty of ideas of Bergson. There are deeper reasons for his public importance.

In order to understand Professor Dewey's thinking, one must go back to fundamentals, though Dewey himself enunciated them only very late in the explicitness of a book. It was not until the publication of 'Experience and Nature' that he laid bare those basic principles of metaphysics and philosophy upon which his own students well knew his educational and social theories were erected. Long before Dewey was recognized as a startlingly radical metaphysician he had been hailed as a reformer of education, a liberal in social and moral thinking. Few except professional students of philosophy knew that this liberalism flowed from a conception of experience and of philosophy, so completely a break from tradition that small wonder it was difficult to find a language in which to say it. Professor Dewey had long been offering the humble but, in academic philosophy, quite heretical suggestion that philosophy was vision, that thinking was a controlled vista of experience and its possibilities, that the central instrument of vision was intelligence and the area of vision all that man is and sees and does and suffers. 'We need,' Professor Dewey was eventually to say in 'Experience and Nature,' 'a cautioning and directive word like experience, to remind us that the world which is lived, suffered and enjoyed, as well as logically thought of, has the last word in all human inquiries and surmises. This is a doctrine of humility, but it is also a doctrine of direction. For it tells us to open the eyes and ears of the mind, to be sensitive to all the varied phase of life and history. Nothing is more ironical than that philosophers who have professed universality have so often been one-sided specialists . . . ignoring ignorance, error, folly, and the common enjoyments and adornments of life.'

The first thing Professor Dewey did, was to take philosophy out of doors and into the open air of public human experience. Within the closets of the professional philosophers it had been babbling its dialectic mysteries, professional secrets which had outside the charmed circle singularly little secular persuasion or importance. Mind and body, purpose and chance, the one and the many, all these were resolved into fantastic verbal solutions of unreal and verbal problems.

Philosophy, as Dewey conceives it, *c'est tout autre chose*. It is a directive vision of common human possibilities. It is an enunciation of the ideals which the conflicts within experience generate, a suggestion of the ways by which intelligence may resolve those conflicts and make the world, through intelligence, a little nearer the clarified heart's desire.

Philosophy, for Professor Dewey, turns, therefore, in two directions, one toward an analysis of that nature which is the matrix of all experience, and, secondly, toward those social and moral situations in which experience becomes meaningful and in which intelligence becomes operative. It is hard to say which side of Professor Dewey's thinking is the more arresting and important. For all that, his popular reputation rests on his educational and social ideas; among philosophers (both those who applaud and those who are made uneasy by him) it is his metaphysical radicalism that is of first importance.

The revolution Professor Dewey has brought about is difficult to explain in a brief article for a lay public. In Dewey's writings themselves the exposition is tangled up with controversial discussions of opposed and traditional posi-

tions. It is complicated by a style not cal-
culated either to seduce or to illuminate those
innocent of the philosophical tradition. More's
the pity! For the leading ideas of this 'instru-
mentalist philosophy' are at once simple and
radical and humane. The chief of them, perhaps, is the call to philosophy to turn to the
whole of experience for its subject matter instead of confining itself to that highly intellectualized and verbal realm which has been the
terrain of philosophers of the past. 'When we
say that history is one point of approach to an
account of the world in which we live we mean
then by experience something at least as wide
and deep and full as all history on this earth,
a history which, since history does not occur
in the void, includes the earth and the physical
relatives of man. . . . Without sun, moon and
stars, mountains and rivers, forest and mines,
soil, rain and wind, history would not be.
These things are not just external conditions
of history and experience; they are integral
with them. But also without the human attitude and interest, without record and interpretation, these things would not be historical.'

It is the business of philosophy as Dewey

conceives it, to study the objective conditions which set the limits of action, the method of intelligence by which those conditions may be propitiously controlled. For Dewey it is a fact of cardinal importance that this is a universe in which thinking occurs. The fact that thinking does occur in it indicates what kind of a universe it is. It is an impressive mixture of stability and precariousness. 'Change gives meaning to permanence, and recurrence makes novelty possible. A world that was wholly risky would be one in which adventure was impossible. Only a living world can include death.' It is because human beings are harassed animals living in a changing world that they are compelled to think to save, and to secure, their lives. It is, on the other hand, because in the apparent and bewildering chaos there are dependable and stable things that thinking is at all possible; it is because there are predictable recurrences, knowables among novelties, that thinking is efficacious.

But further than this: Experience is a process and a process takes time. Or, in one of Dewey's rare apothegms, 'Every existence is an event.' It is often observed that Bergson was the first one to insist on the importance of time in philosophy. But it is doubtful whether time is used by Bergson as radically and as pivotally as it is by Dewey. To the latter the whole of the natural scene, including its human inhabitants, may be said to be a moving picture. Things may be said to occur rather than to be. This spectacle of perpetual occurrences and perpetual changes is not simply desolation and tragedy, as it has been held to be by the drooping moralist or sighing poet. Rather, human hopes lie precisely in that unfinished and adventurous history, to the future course of which their own coöperating intelligence (itself a function of nature) may make a difference.

To the study of the functioning of intelligence in society, politics and education Professor Dewey has devoted many years of careful analysis. His whole theory of life may be said to revolve around his pivotal notion of thinking. Left to random impulse or routine habit, action tends to become mechanical and brutal. Thinking, 'the dramatic rehearsal in imagination' of the consequences of possible acts, keeps life free, flexible and experimental. What is more, it charges the simplest doings of existence with significance. It turns the heavy lethargy of habit, the momentary excitement of the senses into events charged with meaning. It transforms the creature of caprice or automatism into an imaginative being who does what he does from choice and whose doings are illuminated with insight.

Professor Dewey's whole social philosophy is concerned with the nurture and emancipation of just such human beings. The doctrine of 'creative intelligence' turns the whole of morals to a new quest. It changes it from an enunciation of absolutes derived from God or dialectic into a clarification of that 'experimental science of living' which would be the only relevant moral thinking. As the physical sciences, in engineering and medicine, have transformed and ameliorated the conditions of life, so moral science, as Professor Dewey envisages it, might make a habitable future for a world now given over to superstitions and traditional violences in the relations of men to one another.

It is with the relations of men to one another that Dewey is primarily, almost Puritanically, concerned. His book, 'Human Nature and Conduct,' makes it clear how much of our action is the function of habit, how much habit is the function of social contacts. If ever action is to be freed from slavish routine or blind and wanton impulse it can be only through what is for Dewey the supreme art, education. That art, as he conceives it, is the process by which a social group insures its own continuous and intelligent reorganization through the inculcation of a habit of free and continuous intelligence in the young. All those hopeful recent experiments in education, schools which are miniature and liberated societies (represented by the Walden School and the City and Country School in New York), owe their impulse in one way or another to Dewey. All that right-about-face which insists now that education be concerned with the living possible future instead of merely transmitting the irrevocable past has Dewey to thank for the prophetic words which gave it stimulus, direction and being.

But Dewey has been always too much of a philosopher to rely on a single instrument, the school, for his hopes of a regenerative society. Behind his social and educational program lies an abounding faith in and a profound conception of democracy. If education is the training of individuals in thoughtful and creative individuality, then any society is estimable to the extent to which it is educative — that is, the degree to which it promotes in its members freedom and creativity and intelligence and vision. It is for this reason that Dewey, possibly the most thoroughgoing democrat in the history of thought, sets such vital store by democracy. By it he means no machinery of universal voting, but a society of vivid, free and universal contacts. We have had but the feeblest shadow of it in politics; in education and industry it has scarcely penetrated. But, this is perhaps Dewey's ultimate faith, it will.

'When,' he says in a passage quoted from 'The Public and Its Problems,' 'the machine age has thus perfected its machinery it will be a means of life and not its despotic master. Democracy will come into its own, for democracy is a name for a life of free and enriching communion. It had its seer in Walt Whitman. It will have its consummation when free social inquiry is indissolubly wedded to the art of full and moving communication.'

Wedded as Professor Dewey has been ostensibly to social and metaphysical analysis, in the long run he comes to a conclusion that moves in the society of symbols and art. It is all the more pity that Dewey's language, save in the rarest instances, has not a touch of positive eloquence. For on this theme, which is indeed the climax and core of his thinking, he is indeed genuinely moving. Life, he insists time and again in that flat but beautifully honest prose of his, is life abundant to the extent that it is rich meaning. Meanings are always suggested in symbols, and symbols are always the province of art. Life itself, to the extent that it is experiment and adventure, directed by imaginative intelligence, is an art. Science, which is the name for a thoroughgoing and disciplined intelligence, is a possible universal art. And the function of religion, apparently so timid and backward-looking in a lost wayward age, is what it always has been, to translate the brute facts and relevant aspirations of human creatures into common and moving symbols. For Dewey, democracy, the matrix of contemporary social life, and science, the method of contemporary living, both have remained up to the present thin, mechanical and external. It remains for the poets and prophets of the future to convert what is as yet new and bare and angular into symbols, the symbols, warm, intimate, and imaginative, of a personal and moving art.

It is a pleasant irony to think that this philosopher, beginning with an abstract analysis of the nature of experience itself, observing its stability and its change, and the saving possibility of intelligence, comes to conclusions that are a poetic and religious apotheosis of democracy and science. For behind the metaphysician in Dewey lies a spirit singularly and simply American in its passion for democracy. Behind the technical controversialist lies a visionary who sees in science the method by which that fair dream of democracy may be realized. Below the jagged prose of a thinker more given to thinking than to music or ornament lies the germ of that poetry and religion which will find its vital and honest source in the honestly faced life of our own day. It is a tribute to the American public that it has long sensed that Dewey stood for all this, without quite understanding why.

WE SUPERSTITIOUS MODERNS

It is a curious comfort to wallow sometimes in the mire of ancient superstitions and to congratulate ourselves that the race has advanced so far beyond the terrors and turbulences of mind and imagination that afflict primitive man. In reading about the varieties of magic and trembling taboos with which our uncivilized ancestors tormented their lives or hoped to preserve them, we like to contrast their unhappy state with our free, sophisticated lot. We reflect that we have substituted clear intelligence for muddled magic, sanity and sense for undisciplined desperation and terror. The history of the human mind, we pleasantly conclude, is an unmistakable progress. It is the increasingly successful attempt to disentangle fact from fancy, to face the world candidly, clearly, and directly, to meet experience in its own terms, to understand the world, and in so far to master it.

Now, it has long ago been noted that superstition is simply an immature and impatient science, a childish attempt to control the world and the fortunes of mankind. Where life is harassed and uncertain, almost any measure will be taken that promises salvation. To give the gods the fairest portion of meat or wheat, to mumble an allegedly potent abracadabra, to promote the fertility of the fields through obscene rites, to slay your enemy by chanting his name or painting his picture or burning his effigy — all these are devices by means of which primitive man has tried to save himself from drought or famine or enemies, to achieve some security in a life full of disturbing realities and imaginations equally disturbing. We read about these pathetic and desperate means whereby a savage tries to save himself or his tribe. We smile with a mingled emotion of relief and superiority and pity. Thank God or civilization, we say, that we are not as they! Or are we?

The most striking feature of the Western world, next, perhaps, to the industrial revolution, is the extent to which a certain minimum of literacy and cultivation is current among men. It would seem that never before have the methods of science or the fruits of scientific method been such common coin among the generality of mankind. The jargon of science, the symbols of intelligence, have never before been so vernacular in men's mouths. And the promise of science, at least in the realm of physical comfort and convenience, has been so extraordinarily well fulfilled that we are ready to listen to any voice that speaks in an ostensibly scientific medium, to have faith in any miracle whose apparatus is ostensibly modern, to be charmed by any spell, so only that it be chanted according to the cadences of the contemporary mumbo-jumbo.

For, so far as essential human nature is concerned, the necessity or comfort of miracles is as genuine as ever. The bliss and perfection of life that Francis Bacon and his fellow-trumpeters of science foresaw, have not, save with respect to the mechanics of life, been fulfilled. We are as much as ever this side of paradise. The physical complication of things has not simplified the problems of our society or of our souls. So far as peace among men or the integrity of the spirit of man is concerned, we are as harassed and helpless as our primitive ancestors. We are as much in need of a miracle to save us as is a savage pursued by a whirlwind. We are as ready to fly to a magic remedy; we are as easily duped by a plausible cure. Human nature remains in its impulses essentially the same, however much by its monstrously altered setting it may be disguised. The magic to which it is susceptible has changed, but it is still susceptible to magic. A troubled soul still flies from the hopeless brutality of a fact to the hope and promise of a new fancy. It is as ready as ever to seek refuge in a miracle, to spy short cuts to salvation.

There is only one antidote to belief in magic, and that is a continuously active habit of criticism and analysis. There is nothing in the conditions of contemporary life or the structure of human nature to make us hopeful that the habit of free and analytic thought is more pervasive than it has been in the past. There continue to operate, on the other hand, precisely the ancient and ineluctable facts of human need and human impatience. Thinking is in its very essence an interruption to behavior; it is the only secure method of solving a problem, but it is halting, tentative, and indirect. It provides solutions ultimately and with a fair degree of certainty, but a promised eventual solution is not a virtue in an emergency, and probability is not a comforting answer to desperation. The urban mind to-day is

as ready as the forest mind of twenty thousand
years ago to turn to a formula, a certainty, a
guaranteed relief and salvation.

The tendency to turn from a candid and
clear-headed dealing with the facts to a mystic
flight into magic and superstition has always
been most rife where disappointment and disillusion have been most current. It was in the
sunset break-up of the Græco-Roman world,
in the disillusion of a civilization going to ruins,
that there was an incredible uprush of half-
buried superstitions, a flight to formulas and
rituals and magic and spells. In a sense our own
situation is parallel.

Like the thinkers of the late Greek world, we
are, in Professor Gilbert Murray's phrase, undergoing a 'failure of nerve.' Intelligence has
revealed to us a great deal, but most of its revelations have been in the way of irony and disillusion. Our literature and our education have
taught us to face facts, but the facts of the last
decade have not taught us to caress the intelligence that revealed them. Like the stricken
multitudes of the ancient pagan world, we look
for a way to be saved. Like tribes of savages,
tormented with drought or deluge, famine or
pestilence, we turn anywhere and everywhere

to be rescued. And, as always, not least to the medicine-man and magicians of our own day.

Our medicine-men and magicians are not so fantastic in their dress, their rites, or their appearance as the medicine-men of old, but they resemble them in several very important ways. One of the great powers of the magician among primitive men was his supposed science and his control of words. And the chief instrument of the magic to which we appeal to-day is to the magic of names. It is by a formula, an incantation, an idea that contemporary magic appeals. It is a single phrase, a single principle, a single method, a single hope upon which we are to rest our salvation. And these single sesames to security, happiness, progress, and peace that rise and fall so rapidly in popular interest and esteem are all bathed in the aura of science. They are supposed knowledge, supposed certainties, in precisely the same way as the taboos and mumbo-jumbo, the fastings and lacerations, of a Fiji-Islander, a Zulu, and a Bushman are supposed accurate methods of control based on an accurate knowledge of the nature of things.

The rise and fall of interest in contemporary intellectual fashions thus has a comparatively simple explanation. Most of the new ideas of the last two decades have been in some way or other scientific in character. Anything that goes under the ægis of science gains a special claim to consideration because of the fact that the methods of science and the laboratory have been the obvious instruments by which the world of externals about us has been revolutionized. It is supposed that the science which has brought about the radio and the rapid transit will be equally useful in solving the ills of social and political life, of a crucified soul, or a hysteric spirit. The layman, even of a professedly intellectual bent and interest, seldom realizes how precarious and tentative are the results of science, and how plodding and piecemeal are its methods. If the miracle of transporting sound thousands of miles without wire may be accomplished, surely the wise men may be believed when they tell us they can order our society, abolish war, glorify our characters, and save our souls. So any hint or whisper of salvation that comes from the quarter called scientific is hailed as a way out, a release, an escape, a philosopher's stone.

Belief in magic in so far as it affects the physical world is easily checked up. An airy

86

theory of weight will not hold up a building, no bridge could be built by an engineer who operated with airy mathematics; but magic with relation to human affairs is easier to believe and harder to check. It is harder to check because its language is vaguer and its specifications more elusive. It is easier to believe because there is more incitement to the human spirit to believe in marvel than to explode or dismiss it. It is not surprising, therefore, that there should have been since the middle of the nineteenth century an extraordinary succession of intellectual fads, of fashionable superstitions in the realm of politics and morals, of psychology and education.

It is natural, in the first place, that thinkers about specifically human problems should have wished to parallel in methods and results an improvement in human affairs such as the methods of science have effected in the realm of things. The attempts to substitute the conception and the methods of the laboratory and the test-tube for those of the propagandist and the dealer in words have indeed been the most hopeful promise in the amelioration of human affairs. But it is equally natural that the polarization of these ideas should as frequently lead to superstition as to enlightenment. What in the hands of a careful and trained inquirer is a mere suggestion, a first hypothesis, an uncertified gleam, becomes among the pseudo-scientific and the intelligent men of the forum a new gospel, a modern decalogue, a healing wind for a stricken world. A faint light thrown on the processes of the ductless glands is made the signal of a new era. Control the thyroid gland, you create a transformed race. A physician in a psychopathic clinic makes some interesting observations on the unconscious factors entering into the lives of his hysteric patients.

Lo! the libido! Hail the unconscious! Behold the grand new insight by which rottenness is to be cleansed out of the human spirit, its complexes to be made simple, the subsoil of its obscenity sublimated into poetry and Platonism and art! Given a few unquestionably real facts about suggestibility and hypnosis, and a provincial French apothecary or a metropolitan press agent, or a combination of both, invents rituals and spells by which the lame are to be made to walk, the blind to see, the dumb to speak.

The vogue of psychoanalysis is peculiarly a case in point. Psychoanalysis originated and is still continued by sincere and systematic inquirers. These men are expert psychiatrists, trying with unspectacular precision to turn up and turn to account some of the pivotal unrecognized factors in human conduct. A new dimension has been added to the understanding of our motives and our actions. Light has been thrown on the darknesses that used to veil motives below the level of consciousness and blind us to the unacknowledged urgencies and compulsions of sex. But psychoanalysis as a fad, an enthusiasm, a cure-all, a redeeming belief, is not science at all, but magic of a peculiarly pernicious sort. For a time it appeared as if the whole literate public were to be marooned forever on the beach of this scarcely charted country. The fact of sex was the pivot of understanding. The terms of a tentative, modest, and infant science became the jargon and shibboleths of a hurried salvation. To be psychoanalyzed was to be saved. On the stream of a freed libido were to be washed away all the uncleannesses of a repressed spirit. The case of the young man aged twenty-seven whose mother was neurasthenic and whose father was polymorphously perverse has, of course, become familiar to any one at all in touch with modern thought. The young man's loss of his job, bad temper at home, and his poor appetite are explained by a bewildering combination of bisexual retrogressions, Œdipus complexes, and anxiety neuroses. Only the probe of the analyst can save him. One may take one's choice of early- or latter-day superstitions: the amateur analyst with his pretentious and complicated formulas, his bated scientific breath, and his ritualistic language, or the more picturesque unction and ceremonies of the savage magician rehearsing his recitatives over his herbs and incense and fire.

There is a similar history to be written of the vogue of glands. Sustained and quiet researches in medical laboratories, notably in the medical schools of Harvard and Columbia Universities, had for years been revealing the fact that the ductless glands in the human body have a significant effect on health, growth, vitality, and, in consequence, on character. But the vogue of glands in allegedly intellectual society in this country is a curious and ironic episode in the history of human culture. A fact was made into a fetish, and a helpful path struck out in medical science was hailed as

a mystic avenue to salvation. What profit it a
man that he be well nourished, well exercised,
well housed, well fed, well paid, well loved, if
the glandular foundations of his life be all
awry? The fad lasted long enough for a novel
and a moving-picture to grow out of one of its
more spectacular phases, the relations of gland
and youth. But given another year, and the
new glandular medicine would have produced
tragedies whose heroes met disaster through
the fatality of a gland more or less, or a gland
more or less out of tune. The day of the economic interpretation was over, and almost as
much a thing of the past were complexes, transferences, projections, and repressions. All
previous miasmas of language made way for
the more summary obscurity of glands. One
daily awaited a 'History of the Human Race in
Terms of Variations in the Thyroid.' There
was many a latter-day believer who thought
the light that never was on sea or land had
been cast by the new glandular medicine on
every secret fastness of the human soul.

To record the history of popular intellectualism in the last two decades would be to record
the history of the rise and fall of successive
faiths, of plausible modern magics, of unex-

amined faiths in unparalleled cures. Some of them are more palpably naïve and absurd than others. But scarcely any was absurd enough not to gain the hospitable attention of scholars who should have been made more circumspect by a long acquaintance with the history of human folly.

The central faith, perhaps, that underlies most of these magics of the new age is the belief in the efficacy of 'psychology.' The natural and plausible inference is that what science has accomplished in the domain of things, it may equally well accomplish in the realm of mind and morals. For every tentative step made in increasing our information about the tangled skein of human motives and human behavior, there are dozens of volumes and hundreds of periodicals engaged in 'putting psychology over' as the new instrument of salvation. In this instance salvation has been put on an efficiency basis. There is a whole new industry devoted to whipping up people's will power, accelerating the fermentation of ideas in their brains, enhancing their personality, teaching them concentration for success. Corporations have been formed for vending will power; forests of white paper have been sacrificed to advertising gospels of success. Every one is familiar with the pointed forefinger directed menacingly at the reader from the back page of a Sunday magazine. Every one knows the strong gray face warning him to buy from this or that incorporated ism or this or that glad psychologist, limited, the simple and unique bunkum that will convert him from a creature of vacillations to an electric current of will to success. The subway news-stands are littered with a bastard crew of magazines ballyhooing brain power, will power, thought power, or personality plus. For fifteen cents the copy one can have chaos turned into character, wobbliness into will, lassitude into dynamics, passiveness into 'pep.' Most of these enterprises are commercial, not least so when they take the form of lectures delivered in luxurious auditoriums of smart hotels. But just as soup is not only made for profit in factories, but given away in soup kitchens, so will power, personality, brains, and success are being given away by benevolence. They are given away as gratis miracles on Tuesday evenings in churches which waning faith has left empty on Sundays. The Tuesday evening magic is not more efficacious, though much less lovely than the old. But the old beliefs are traditional; they are frayed, suspect, and outworn. The new beliefs of the glad psychologists have the tang and relevance of modernity; their promise is not that of hypothetical bliss in the next world, but of success in the vale of here and now. And as among primitive tribes the most passionate prayers and deliberate rites are not for distant and dubious happiness in another world, but for wind or rain or food in this. The crowds that pay for the will-power magazines, that come to personality lectures in ball-rooms or in churches, are hungering for cashable miracles, bigger and better jobs, better places in society. Hence the sale found for these short cuts to bliss provided by what Everett Dean Martin has well described as 'scamp psychologists.' A large-scale business has been made out of the ancient and agreeable superstition that beggars who wish hard enough may ride. Strong language is supposed to bring about strong will, glad words, glad tidings. Babies alone are supposed to point to the moon and cry because they cannot reach it. But a whole trade and whole fortunes have been built up in selling the idea that by buying certain particular rituals, mumbling specific iterations (cf. 'Every day in every way'), the moon may really be had.

But interest in the life to come has likewise stimulated a latter-day science of superstition. This is not the first time in the history of civilization that another world has seemed to be the only decent refuge from this one, whose most palpable essence is disaster. The war made death so sudden and brutal a fact in the lives of thousands that any voice that brought tidings of a hereafter was not to be disregarded. During the visits of Sir Oliver Lodge to this country it was notable how many among his audiences were people in mourning. The same impulses that of old made people seek for immortality are still with us. These impulses now seek a rational justification in something more substantial than faith and more cogent than eloquence. What is no longer susceptible of proof by argument or homily now seeks assurance through photography. Ectoplasm seeks to prove what can no longer be demonstrated by dialectics. Along with scientific breakfast food and scientific will power, one can have now, for the asking, scientific immortality.

In the past the tendency toward a flight from this world has usually been accompanied by an abdication of the only instrument that promised betterment of its conditions, reason or intelligence. The cool counsels of analytic intelligence preached by Aristotle in healthy days of Athenian thought was in the decadence of the third century A.D. superseded by a preaching of mysticism by a rapturous flight from the alone to the alone. A similar counsel finds many voices in this generation, not least in the able and persuasive writings of Bergson. For a time this thinker experienced a vogue that would never have been made possible by the highly technical character of his writings themselves. But there was enough clarity in his writings and enough energy in his disciples to make clear the drift and momentum of his teachings. And they were teachings not unamiable to a generation looking for a way out or a way home. The way to salvation and truth, so said this thinker and his disciples, was not intelligence, which was a frozen analysis of death, a *rigor mortis* of ideas. Through impulses alone one touched reality, and instinct alone led one to the truth. An uprush of intense feeling was a more massive and reliable guide than cool-headed discrimination. To feel one's own pulse beat, to sense the tremor

of truth that was the soul of one's passion, was
to confute the death's-head of intellectualism.
Most seductive of all in Bergson's attack on
science was the atmosphere of science in which
it moved. No one has ever more subtly at-
tacked subtlety or with more adroit intelligence
shown the limits of intelligence itself. Where
Bergson led, hundreds of lesser men have been
avid to follow. The same spirit has found mul-
tiform expression in the hundreds of varieties
of New Thought, of avenues to the larger life,
of aids to the creative spirit that fill on Sunday
afternoons private houses on New York's upper West side, or hotels and theaters and
women's clubs throughout the country. To be
simple in a complex cosmos, spontaneous in a
mechanical world, to be naïve in the midst of
sophistication — these are the simplest of all
the new and simple ways of being saved. Become simple as a little child, and the kingdom
of heaven is at hand.

One might thus pursue indefinitely the
theme of mythology under the guise of science,
and attractive shams that have gone in the
clothes of certainty. People have, of course,
fled to miracles always in the genuine hope
that they would work. They fly from them as

quickly when it is discovered that they don't. In the ancient, unhappy days a magician whose wares did not work was punished with exile or torture or death. In our society he is simply punished with oblivion. People are too eager to read or hear about the latest cure to remember that the last one was a fraud or a failure or both. By the time the new cure is under way in its public career, the old one is so far forgotten that it is even forgotten that it did not work. There is more enticement in a new untried promise than in one that is a year old and is tried and broken.

One might describe the literate world to-day as experiencing a pervasive neurasthenia. A great madness has fallen upon us, an impatience of the slow processes of intelligence along with a glib use of its language. Through the instruments of science we have built up a mechanical and industrial civilization in which our souls become dazed, if not lost. So, in the long war between the forces of light and darkness, we are tempted to play the defeatist part. In the face of an unprecedentedly complex world, we seek a fee simple to happiness. It may be because our hopes of an ordered and organized world have been rendered ironic and irrelevant by the international chaos of the last decade. But because directed and controlled inquiry has not solved our difficulties, it should at least be clear, from the history of once credited magic, that no magic will.

In the face of an extraordinary uprush of superstition (nearly always in the past an expression of age of despair), perhaps the one legitimate counsel would be that of skepticism. Skepticism may easily turn into cynicism or revolt. It may paralyze action. It may, on the other hand, be the indispensable beginning of wisdom and the prerequisite to relevant action. To distrust myth is not to distrust method. It is the substitution of intellectual patience for a rash credulity.

The essence of superstition is to believe in effects without causes, in achievements without the mechanisms for attaining them. And the tragic feature of such beliefs is that faith in a miracle renders uninteresting any search or encouragement of search for means by which the desired results sought for might be prosaically and certainly achieved. Perhaps it is because the methods of science, of criticism, of analysis, of inquiry, of hypothesis, and of testing are so slow, so halting and in essence so un-

99

certain that the modern believer has rushed to shams that have the glamour of speed and certainty and ease. Perhaps the human spirit cannot live in a world without guaranties. Perhaps experience is so discouraging or so disordered that nothing but a miracle can save us. But ours are not likely to be more efficacious than were the shabby and exploded wisdoms of an elder and simpler day.

It is a commonplace of modern psychiatry that hysterical patients live in a world of their own imagined creation, a smooth delirium in which all their difficulties are, in imagination, solved. But the temporary flight to these comfortable phantasies makes these poor deranged creatures less than ever the masters of their tattered destinies. The pleasant delirium of their dreams makes their actual lives no less a nightmare. It ought by this time to be a commonplace that the hysterical solutions which have in the last two decades been current for saving the world have a similar effect; they corrupt the very moral fiber and intellectual temper by which, if at all, the conditions of life may be improved. But perhaps the appearance on earth of a race that could bear to face nature and life without recourse to some form or other of magic would itself be a miracle.

THIRTY SPEAKS TO TWENTY

THE HIGH CHAIR SPEAKS TO THE PERAMBULATOR

DEAR FREDERICK:

I feel I have something special to say to you that I am, perhaps, by age peculiarly placed to say, that you may, perhaps, be not unwilling to hear. You and I can still understand each other; at thirty I have still most of your enthusiasms and passions; at thirty I still hear myself sometimes described as a young man. The middle-aged still seem to me, as they seem to you, stuffy and settled. With you I still want to make, I still believe the world can be made something closer to the clarified heart's desire. There are all sorts of illusions, sweet, persistent and foolish by which we both still live. Love is one of them, I think, though I hardly believe in its eternity any longer, as I suspect you do. That old spoilt child of eighteenth-century reason is another, the perfectability of human nature. And, when digestion is in order (as alas at thirty it is not always) I think I share, though more quietly, your own sensibility to the colors and shapes of the world about you. Years of concert going have not withered nor staled my excitements about music. While I resent the displacement of travel more than I used to, you will recall seeing me not infrequently at the art exhibitions last year.

While I am not as hopeful as you seem to be, of any new scheme of salvation that creeps into the public consciousness, I have not been so shattered by scepticisms but that I still warm to any movement, liberal and hopeful, that any prophet or propagandist may launch upon our time. Friends constitute still part of the delightful furniture of heaven and earth, though I have lost some by death, and others by default, on their part or on my own. And I do not make friends, I find, as easily as I used to, as freely as you still do.

In all these major respects, I think we are of the same fraternity, if not of quite the same generation. But ten years make a difference, and I suspect the last ten years have made a greater difference than a decade usually can create. There are the perpetual differences between twenty and thirty of which I hardly need to remind you. If you do not know them, you will find them out for yourself in ten years or so. Life at thirty can scarcely be said to be over. I have not wasted my soul nor my substance, having, perhaps, not too much of either to waste. With good luck, there are doubtless any number of pleasant possibilities that the world still holds open. But none the less at thirty, one begins to look back, like Marcel Proust, at 'le Temps Perdu.' Unless one has the genius for salvaging it by putting it into a book, there is much of the last ten years that to a thirty-year-old man, will appear blind effort or effortless waste. There are the things he might well have done and did not do. The things it is quite too late to regret doing. Regret, Spinoza insists, is a wasteful emotion, and here in this August sunlight in the mountains a thousand feet above a Swiss lake, regret seems strangely trivial and irrelevant. But one does have regrets that at your age (as I write this suddenly, you do seem very young) you cannot have. Heaven knows I have seen you waste time and waste emotion. But hardly long enough to have it matter very much. In the long run you will have profited by most of it, and it can all be set down to experience. There is still lots of time to learn better. Your elders know that and forgive you for your as yet unbroken promise. You know it yourself, and life is full of too much color and glamour to give you much pause to care whether you know it or not. When some escape or some detour turns out to be quite blind and futile, you have always the comfort of knowing, that, like a musician, with a fertile and vivacious theme, you can start another variation. At thirty, one knows, one's friends know, that the theme is less fertile than one thought it, and one cannot forever start anew.

That difference of perspective, I think, indicates the dates that lie between us. Once I told you that I had been in my present profession ten years. You replied in some amused surprise that you had been doing nothing as yet for ten years. You are still perplexed and stimulated by the possible. At thirty much of the perplexity and the excitement of it will have vanished. You will have found your field to furrow or your garden to cultivate. You will hate it or love it, but you will be perforce acquiescent. You will, to use one of your own favorite expressions, be considerably less high hat about your world.

But if I may continue to remind you of things of which I said you needed no reminder, the chief differences between us lie within the limits of our resemblances. I said at thirty I still believe in all the old and saving illusions, love and friendship and the perfectibility of human nature and each new cause, as hopeful, as touching, as doomed as the story of any human life. I believe in them, however, with a difference. To say indeed that I believe in them is a kind of falsity. I am still young enough to be susceptible to them. I long ago, however, discovered all the things about them that trouble you in the very temple of your delight. You fly from ecstasy to disenchantment. Now love gilds your world completely, and now you perceive the emptiness of the gilt. Now love is a winged spirit, now it is a gross biological illusion. With those sometimes eloquent lips of yours with which you swear it is eternal, you know — how many poets of our day have told you — that it is scarcely even temporary. It is defeasible not simply by death but by distraction. People do not simply die; they move away. The three or four Springs of your adolescence have taught you much of the cynical wisdom of the ages on this theme so salty and so sweet. At thirty, unless human nature changes as rapidly as the radio and the aeroplane, you will be both less lyrical and less cynical. You will be able to love, indeed you will still have to love. But you will not have to or want to talk about it with the hardness of the cynic or the rapture of the fool. I suspect you may not want to talk about it at all.

As to the perfectibility of human nature — even in this age of sophistication, you still believe in that, though its instrument is not God or salvation, but psychoanalysis or glandular secretions or some still more fashionable modern nostrum. It is only stupidity or special interest, you insist, that makes our world such a chaos. I know how much you feel that. I have seen you standing against my bookcase, one elbow resting on a bust of Socrates, the other disarranging a set of Gibbon, while you poured out your sense of how easy it would be to have a tidy ordered cosmos. Once you brought a friend with you who was not so sure. He had been reading some of the modern futilitarians by whom, I notice, you yourself are beginning to be touched. He went to the other extreme, this youth, and insisted that nothing could be done, and that if it could, how did anybody know it was worth doing.

At thirty my generation particularly has

lost its fantastic faith of before the war, and the fantastic melancholy into which you and your sad young companions have fallen. I told you some paragraphs back there was a peculiar difference between us. There is, and it is the war, responsible, or held to be so, for so many curious and deplorable features of our post-war world. It is impossible to believe as firmly as you in any covenant or instrument that will outlaw war, the method, so to speak, that will permanently legalize happiness. Remember, my contemporaries and I were just a little under twenty when the war broke out. That impact shattered our facile little Utopias. But we have lived to see the world go on after all the muck and agony and disillusion. We cannot or will not allow ourselves to ask as many questions about purpose and futility as you do.

At thirty one has lived long enough to see hopes foundered and enthusiasms wrecked in the lives of one's self and one's friends. One has lived long enough, too, to have gained some respect for the paradoxical persistence, the incredible vitality of life. One still believes in possible worlds. Perhaps to cease to have that happy animal faith is to cease to live. Perhaps having it is what makes me side with you as over against middle age where these slightly aging bones of mine begin to tell me I belong. It is not that I have given up asking ultimate things about life. But at thirty one begins to appreciate Samuel Butler's salty remark, 'Is life worth living? That is a question for an embryo, not for a man.'

We differ, too, in our enthusiasms for the things of the senses and the arts. I envy you your appetite. We dined together, you remember, about a month ago. I begrudged you your ability to eat lobster and ice cream and drink nearly a whole bottle of wine. I pride myself on being an Epicurean, but, as the French say, *en detail*. I admire your perfectly rabid hunger for sensations. Mine is more moderate. If I have studied physiology to any account, yours will be. It is not simply the difference in our physique. There is a fundamental difference, I think, in our philosophy of sensation. Especially in that refined form of it which is our passion for the arts. You have been reading Pater, I suspect, and like most sensitive young men, have been seduced by his Conclusion to the Renaissance, 'To burn always with a hard gem-like flame, to maintain this ecstasy is success in life.' Well, in the first

108

place, it cannot be done. Thirty can tell you; forty, I suspect, could underline it. And there are other kinds of success, more rich and more enduring. Beauty is still for you a kind of escape from a distressing world that does not come up to your adolescent specifications. You wish to retire into it, as into a marble and lucid monastery. You will learn very likely, and soon enough, that you do not wish to live in a monastery, and you will have a family and a profession to entangle you deliciously or excitingly or depressingly in something else than the Quest for Beauty and the pure fire of sensation. You will less and less want to live like a stanza out of Edna St. Vincent Millay.

I say this with a conviction born of an experience you cannot have had, precocious youngster though you are. Adolescence is the great egotistic period not simply because it is the age when a personality begins to be acutely, often agonizingly aware of itself. It is the period of egotism because the conditions of life are, despite the pressure of teachers and preachers and family, relatively independent. You are tied by the glamorous loose knots of adolescent love and the bonds, rhetorically eternal, actually so loose and light, of adolescent friendship. But you are free as yet of the tight obligations of matrimony and a career. The more fortunate among you can think of life as the material for an exquisite soliloquy of sensation, simply the colloquies, the dialogues, the drama in which willy nilly life will involve you. From twenty to thirty is on the whole the time when the nets of living will enmesh you. You may try to steer clear of them; that is the great testimony that they exist. Even if you resolutely avoid matrimony, or if some inherited wealth enables you to avoid a business or profession, that later independence will be quite a different thing, less spontaneous, less genuinely lyrical than your brooding years of adolescence. The pressures of a family or of professional failure or absorption or success may indeed make the arts delightful momentary escapes for you. Music and poetry and fiction may be for you melodious escapes from life. But I suspect something healthier may have happened to you before you are thirty. You will come to disesteem a beauty born out of a tinkling concern with the exquisite. You may ask of the arts that they be the adult expression of the interests complex and humane of adult human beings. You will forgive even bad prose and bad drawing when they have something to say.

Something to say? I know it is one of the convictions, possibly only literary, of your generation that there is nothing to be said, save disillusion, nothing to be loved save pleasure, and that with disdain. As a result much of your poetry is a cross between a shrug and a heartbreak. Much of your prose is a sardonic contempt for your own ecstasies. That brings me to another difference between us, which is, I think, to be laid somehow to the quality of the last ten years rather than to the eternal difference that the ten years after adolescence are bound to make. You are wise — so many of your generation are — with a wisdom not your own, if I may so put it. You are wise with the disaffecting insight of the smart young writers whose smartness was turned to gall by the war and its postlude. You are the well informed victims of a consciousness bred of a psychological science, young but dogmatic, that has arisen in the last two decades. I think how naïve we young men were ten years ago. When I hear you, with your bright-eyed nonchalance, quietly dragging masochism and sadism and Œdipus complexes into discussions of religion,

I am a little startled. We thirty-year-olds certainly do date. When I hear the convivial frankness with which you discuss contraception at parties and homosexuality at teas, I feel like the rather blushing ghost of a dead world. I was, if you will permit me, one of the brighter boys at college, but there are a thousand things of which you know and which, what is more, you speak of, which in my day — my bones begin to creak again — we did not know, or if we did, were slightly more diffidently uttered.

I respect all your new information and your new frankness. But your hasty bits of information have led you into one serious error; your passionate desire to be frank has led you — forgive me — to be foolish. For the fact is this new psycho-science about which you gabble so blithely is none too solid at best, and in your hands not a little questionable and thin. And it is not so much your error in detail as your error in direction that troubles me for you. These new terms and shady insights of yours are used not so much to explain as to explain away things. A mother complex is enough for you to destroy all reverence or curiosity about the beautiful legend of the

112

Virgin. When you murmur in your fresh young voice about the Father Image, you think you have said all there is to be said about God. When you babble about infantile fixations, you are certain you have done with the subject of love, though you know well enough that next week you will be quoting Shelley or Keats on the subject to some young thing who is probably more interested in you than either the poets or the psychoanalysts.

Don't be alarmed. I am not going to end by calling you back to God and to Love and to Faith. I have thought about these things enough to suspect those words are veiled with a thousand images, of tradition and prejudice, which make them suspicious to you as to me. I am not old enough or insolent enough yet to attempt to offer you any final and oracular wisdom. I can offer you a firsthand report from the bend, as it were, in the road which you have not yet passed. Thirty has lost its raptures and its disillusions, but not necessarily its spirit. It is, I suspect, the age at which one has begun to grow up. You will, I hope, see that when you get there, with your, no doubt, still interested eyes.

ANTIDOTES

RELIGION FOR THE FAITHLESS

The sea of faith
Was once, too, at the full,
And round earth's shore,
Lay like the folds of a bright girdle furled,
But now I only hear
Its melancholy long withdrawing roar
Retreating to the breath
    Of the night wind, down the vast edges drear
    And naked shingles of the world.

WHEN Matthew Arnold wrote these mournful lines, he was worried because the new science had made it impossible to believe in the old theology; the avalanche of new information was making the old credulities impossible. He was writing in the period when the warfare between science and theology was at its height. On the one hand was the theological picture of a wise, tender, and omnipotent God, ruling the universe in the interest of a fallen but redeemable angel, man. Science was carefully constructing a landscape full of sardonic contrast, a mechanical universe in which blind matter rolled on its relentless way, and man appeared a brief fated flare of dust in a meaningless cycle of destruction. Honest, sensitive, and troubled

minds like Matthew Arnold's engaged in the
thankless — and hopeless — task of reconcil-
ing these irreconcilables. They tried to make
the sweet incredible mysteries of theology con-
sonant with the hard unquestionable teaching of
science. The furies of that old conflict have not
died down. There are still fundamentalists on
both sides. But the conflict and the reconciliations now, after fifty years, both seem strangely
ancient. It seems trivial now to adjust Darwin
and Genesis to each other. In the tumult of
clashing ideas, religion itself seems to have been
forgotten.

The quarrel between the two rival pictures
of the world given by religion and science has
come to seem as irrelevant to religion, in its intimate and vital sense, as a dissertation on the
history of marriage would be to a person in
love. Religion as an experience is more like
love and rapture than it is like logic. It is a
sense of dependence arising out of human need,
a hunger for union emerging out of human loneliness, a thirst for salvation arising from frustration and the need for peace. Out of the
expression and exuberance, the failure and
triumphs of human experience, the religious
geniuses of the world have imagined symbols.

They have made banners for the spirit to follow, patterns by which men might passionately and completely live.

The heat of controversy is over, and in the afterquiet of our noisily acquired freedom we are beginning to realize that the human needs out of which religion grows are present as of old, and that the religious experience is untouched and unkillable by the new science. What is permanently relevant in religion is as permanent and true as ever. What it furnishes is as much as ever a need of the human spirit, and something which science cannot provide.

The first step in reverting to the relevant in religion is to give up regarding it as an antiquated competitor of science. In a beautiful metaphor of Everett Dean Martin's, 'religions are not maps of another world.' They are flags on which the human spirit has blazoned its hopes and its idealisms, its passionate acceptances and its serene negations. In their religious beliefs men have written down, as it were, in capital and eternal letters, the conditions under which the spirit of man must live in the world, and the ideals toward which that spirit moves.

From this point of view, the history of religion becomes a stirring record of the most serious form of the human imagination. It is the story of those metaphors of life and destiny by which whole nations and succeeding generations of men have lived. Each religion, in its dreamed and fanciful world, has given expression to the desires of men, their sense of the ineluctable limits of desire, and their vision of perfection. Their heavens and hells have been anagrams of the spiritual biography of the human soul. Their prayers and sacrifices have been articulations of human impotence and need.

Each religion has its congenial secret and its poetic rendition of the eternal moods and changeless difficulties of mankind. Men, for example, have always been impressed with the rising current of birth and vitality, the languishing tide of death, the certain coming of life again. There are the Dionysiac mysteries of early Greek religion, in which worshipers found vent for the enthusiasm flowing in their own veins, and flowing, too, in the universe, as they saw it in the fresh and green of every spring.

Checked by an experience, where youth grows old, beauty tarnishes, the limbs grow feeble and the mind grows dim, men have always bethought themselves of an eternity of beauty which death cannot defeat or age decay. Out of these imaginings came the Olympian gods, all celerity and clarity, endless coolness and light, beautiful visions of timeless things projected on the screen of time.

Or again, no sensitive mind can go through to maturity without having at some moments a vivid perception of the illusions and delusions of life, a longing for nothingness and a tortured hunger for peace. Buddhism meets this need with its answering doctrine of universal suffering and universal pity, and its assurance of a possible escape into calm and Nirvana. In the field of moral experience, that eternal distinction — inexpungeable to many temperaments — between good and evil was by the Hebrew prophets converted into a flaming injunction delivered for and from an unswerving and righteous God.

But most familiarly in the western world, Christianity has come with its tender and relieving message. Almost everything that the human heart greets or falters from in its passage from birth to death, finds its echo in the Christian story. It has held a promise of salvation to souls, deeply convicted (as who has not been at some moment in his career) of being lost in the world. It has made vivid to millions a Heavenly Father on whom the helpless and undeserving children of flesh might with assurance call. In the face of the bitterness, tawdriness, and corruptions of earthly days, it has taught with persuasive certainty the reality of the City of God, an eternal realm of light and felicity where the soul might find its rest.

These myths and symbols, written by poets with the cosmos for their theme, have, through churches and traditions, widely affected the imaginations and profoundly affected the conduct of millions of people for centuries on our planet. They are looked at askance by the cool objective mind, informed with the jargon of the laboratory and the telescope. But however informed and cool the mind of the modern man, no amount of intellectual denial will destroy his heart or still its longings. That — as Unamuno, the Spanish philosopher, points out — is the tragic irony of our intellectual situation. Our mind remains unsatisfied with the answers needed by our hearts. Our heads are filled with physical science and evolution.

There is no room in them for God, freedom, and immortality. We are too crammed with knowledge to have an empty corner for faith.

To deny that religion is possible any longer because we know too much about the world, is like denying that love is possible because we are learned in sex, or that hunger still exists because we know about calories in food. That sense of mystical union with a universe overwhelmingly larger than and inclusive of ourselves has for many people been the beginning and the core of religious experience. That sense, no mere tinkering with formulæ and slide rules can destroy. The occasional sense of absorption by the whole movement and engulfing splendor of things is shared by the most informed scientist with the most terrified savage. Science, too, leaves the universe as dark and beautiful a mystery as ever. Humility is no less enforced by the vast spaces and atomic complexity of the solar system than it is by a tight little Ptolemaic world. A sense of divinity is provoked by the godlike reaches of the human mind no less than by the traditional name of a personal God.

Religion, indeed, has always been an assertion, romantic and quenchless, that the spirit

counted more than matter, life more than
death, human idealism more than mechanical
defeat. It has frankly been concerned with the
imagined good. It has always built a heaven
whose materials were the heart's desire. We
still imagine goods and our hearts still desire.
Men in their religions have always been devoted to what they conceived to be most serious and important in their lives. Nothing else
is worthy to be called divine; and to live for
the goods, values, and truths which seem
central, beautiful, and enduring is to live truly
for godliness. To be loyal to these is to have
faith in the God that lives actually, where alone
gods have truly dwelt, in man's heart. In the
world, as at present conceived by science, there
is more need than ever for faith in that divinity
which man touches in dreams, and sometimes,
in genius or in rapture, touches in fact. That
divinity is constantly threatened, to use the
old church parlance, by the flesh and the world.
The winged spirit which is man's warrant to
divinity is threatened always by corruption.
Worship of divinity involves, as of old, sacrifice
and it involves prayer. In primitive religions
savage gods demanded material sacrifice for
physical benefits to come. But the symbolic

truth of sacrifice remains. Every loyalty to a good necessarily involves a choice, a negation, a surrender. No artist devoted to creation, no worker devoted to his work, no one who heeds the voice of his hidden but authentic god that dwells in him, but must in some sense deny the world; though no self-respecting mind would any longer expect a self-respecting god to interrupt the machinery of the universe for a man's provincial little petition. But that hush and meditation that come with any attempt to be clear about what one really wishes and what one regards as divine, make prayer no less a beautiful and real thing than of old. The human imagination must always speak in metaphors, and the metaphors of old prayers often serve as well as any. We will say as ever, 'Let the words of my mouth and the meditations of my heart be acceptable in thy sight, O Lord, my strength and my redeemer.' But the God will be a god that dwells in us.

Faith in the divinity immanent in and possible to life has all the compulsions of religion. It requires devotion to the type of life that will preserve those values we are content to call godly. It will mean, as of old, a refusal to bend the knee to Mammon; it will mean the giving up of many a momentary dear pleasure or de-light. One may love beauty and worship truth, but it requires an active piety to make them prevail in the world. In a not too far-fetched sense, to live in the constant companionship of these, and to act toward their realization, is to make the will of God prevail.

It may be protested that only a naïve faith in a personal God can give the unhesitant fervor and the certain peace that go with traditional religion. A mere sense of the generous vitality of nature and the challenging possibilities of life, it will be said, is not enough to fill the needs met by the ancient creeds. It appears to me a very questionable assumption that because faith changes its object, faith no longer endures. For imaginative and sensitive minds, the passion called religious may find another object than the traditional image of God. Any intense allegiance or adventurous devotion is a faith. The artist in his creation, the worker in his work, the teacher in his teaching, if they are sincere and reflective of what they are doing, are performing acts of piety to the commands of an inner god. Permanent and stirring dreams constitute a heaven; a compelling and engrossing ideal is a god. To live governed by these invariables, to make no compromise where they are concerned, is to lead something like what the theologians would call the spiritual life.

This faith in the exuberance of nature and the inventive power of life will not, it is true, give peace. There is no heaven to look forward to save such as we keep shining in our own minds as patterns for the modeling of our lives; there is no power to rely on save those in nature and in ourselves. Faith becomes an adventurous and eager hypothesis. It is belief in the possible conversion of the dream that animates us into living fact. No one that looks before and after can live without some such implicit hope. Without it, life is a dying from moment to moment. The world is certainly far from resembling that picture of its possible loveliness that is carried as the City of God in the head of every idealist. But faith in the dear beauty of that picture is, for generous minds, a religion. Many free minds have had no other.

This faith may be considered merely a form of lyric romanticism rather than a creed. It may be objected that the absurdity of life, the finality of death, are capable of killing any response sufficiently resilient and universal to be called religious. But the religion of the future, while it will certainly have to start from the facts of mechanism and biology, will certainly rise, as religions have always risen, to those peaks and goals of experience on which the eyes of the religious genius have always been fixed. No amount of checkmating by the facts will stop that soaring of the human spirit, or kill its vision of a dreamed-of divinity. That soaring is itself sufficient testimony of the reality of the divine. In merely dreaming of perfection the mind acknowledges its God. In fostering that dream in action, even the faithless will be performing an act of faith. And living among constant goods, imperishable beauties, and invariable truths, the soul, as religions have always promised, will be saved.

ART FOR PHILISTIA

IN that wave of revealing introspection that
has swept over American literature in the last
few years, we have had discovered to ourselves
by writers as different as Sherwood Anderson
and Sinclair Lewis that American life suffers
from standardization, mediocrity, and exter-
nality. We have learned that the American
scene offers no place or shelter for eternal and
beautiful things, and, what is worse, no stimulus or encouragement to the kind of life that
flowers into art. We have been told till it hurts
that we are lost in the morasses of mechanism,
industrialism, and materialism. We have been
convicted of wallowing in haste, waste, and
greed. There has been comparative silence as
an answer to the charges that there is nothing
in our continent or in our civilization that gives
a characteristic savor or meaning or loveliness
to our lives.

Now any one who has traveled much abroad
knows that what these writers say is wrong
with the American scene, has been more or less
wrong with the world since the industrial re-

volution. Much of the joy that an American finds in Europe is not the glamour of a beautified present, but the halo of a dying past. The loveliness is that of individual relics and monuments lingering in the midst of a civilization not much less mechanical or external than our own. The illusion of difference comes partly, though not wholly, from the fact that the American remembers a distilled and purified Europe upon his return. He recalls, not the factories and unemployment of Birmingham but the promenaders in the wide spaces of the Tuileries Gardens. He remembers, not the grime of Manchester but the green of Salisbury, not the soot of the Five Towns but the thatched cottage and the cathedral close.

The indictment that sensitive and creative minds make against the conditions of American life is thus not an accusation against America; it is a charge against that industrial revolution whose operations and consequences are most clearly seen in America where, since it is a young country, there is so little of the lovely persistence of older and more beautiful vestiges and ways of life. The troubled critics of the American scene are making practically the same charges that Matthew Arnold was elegantly thundering against the British middle class fifty years ago. The comfortable citizenry was living upon the fruits of a terrible and dwarfing labor. It was spending its energies in an equally terrible and footless leisure.

Our own recent critics have, on the whole, been concerned not with the hardnesses of the labor on which our civilization rests, but with the rottenness, dullness, and absurdity of the leisure which it makes possible. The industrial millennium has not arrived. But what depresses those concerned for the future of our life on this side of the Atlantic is what that millennium would be like if it did arrive. They have their suspicions, drawn largely from an observation of what preoccupies the time of those economically on the yonder side of Paradise. Lewis Mumford in his striking 'Story of Utopias' points out that the implicit and controlling ideal of our civilization is the Country House, with all that it implies of the way life should be lived. If the measure of our civilization is to be found by what we do or would wish to do with our leisure, we are convicted, most of the critics assure us — and with painfully accurate justice — of doing with it nothing or worse than nothing. They insist that the tempo of our life is Philistine, and that it lacks the quality, the presence, or the possibility of art. Our leisure is as regimented as our labor. Our amusements are as compulsory and as standardized as our work. It is not golf they object to, but the whole regimental rigmarole of the country club. They do not bemoan the radio, but the jazzy disintegration of the radio programs. It is not that we are pressed and penniless; but that having, by current standards, the major wealth and leisure of the world, we live in luxurious barracks, find pleasure in excited and standardized revues, and have neither the individual passion of producing nor the private peace of enjoying art.

For these critics, art and beauty have indeed become the new religion. Having nothing much left to believe in the way of a world to come, they look for something to cling to in the world about them. In the middle of the nineteenth century, along with those optimistic giants of reason, Comte and Mill, we might have evolved for ourselves sufficient faith and exuberance in the possibilities of progress to have founded and found spiritual satisfaction in a religion of humanity. The war — and the peace — have disillusioned us.

The prophets of sensitive despair have fled to the ivory tower. In the exquisite cultivation of beautiful moments, they have found the only hope of grace in a graceless world. The concert hall has become the new cathedral, in which sounds without meaning have been found to be the only pure pleasures in a meaningless world.

But those who flee to art have a profounder reason. They have shaken off the rusty shackles of old foolish moralities, and they have, in a latter day paganism, discovered anew the Greek identity between the beautiful and the good. What is good is not what was commanded by a law no longer believed in. What is good is what is moving to the senses, emotions, and the mind. For art comes to us, in Pater's famous phrase, 'proposing frankly to give nothing but the highest quality to our moments as they pass, and simply for those moments' sake.' And in the perfect moments of pure pleasure in color, word or sound, or the free and perfect spontaneity of artistic production, prophets of the newest paganism see not only a stimulation but a morality, not merely a pleasure but a religion.

Meanwhile the average man in the street

has become increasingly suspicious of and insensitive to art as a thing, a life, a cult. There is no question that in America, for many intelligent minds, art is a foolish epithet adored by effeminate sillies. It is associated with museums that one never enters and books that one never — voluntarily — reads. It is profound, unctuous, and essentially unimportant. It is as serious as a religious service, and as dull. Or it is an embroidered dissipation indulged in by elegant wastrels. It suggests the sultry nonsense of the *fin de siècle* and the worst of Oscar Wilde. The wholesome, normal, full-blooded he-man with the tangible goods of swift motors, week-end golf, and the rattat intoxication of jazz, sniffs at museums, concert halls, and libraries with all their dull and deadly arts. If he tolerates art at all, it is with the breeziest of the intellectuals in their canonization or the lively arts of jazz, vaudeville, and the comic strip.

The wholesome hearties who feel the futility of much irrelevant prettifying that passes for art, are expressing a certain justice in their reactions. Many who produce or are absorbed in the fine arts in our generation are having the experience, not of art, but of day-dreaming.

Art for Philistia

When poetry degenerates into a thin playing with irrelevant verbal music, it is not an art but a tinkling escape from the major concerns of life. It is a flight to phantoms and arabesques from a civilization left no less brutalized and unadorned. Nothing could be more wan and depressing than an evening spent with a group of people whose only concerns are with the choice between mauve color and rose, and who have no life outside the exquisite titillations of the fine arts. Their passions seem puerile and their subject matter nil. One understands why Bernard Shaw believes that in a really adult civilization, like that pictured in the last part of 'Back to Methuselah,' art would take its place along with other toys proper to children. The Sancho Panzas of our day are not complete fools, no more so than was their original. They know there are more important concerns for living men than the tinkle of a rhyme or the last nuance of a color. They are justly suspicious of those who think there are not.

Yet one can believe that in the quarrels between the æsthetes and the hearties, the meaning of art in its widest human sense has been forgotten. They have both failed to see in art that which has made the most profound and vertebrate of thinkers, from the Greeks down, find in it the type and pattern of civilized achievement. They must both fail to understand why these same thinkers have found that a civilization without beauty was not a civilization at all. Oddly enough, the call to art as the type of perfect experience and perfected life has come most urgently in our generation from one not an æsthete at all. It is Havelock Ellis, after a lifetime of frank and mellow survey of all the depths and radiations and heights of human passion, who has pleaded for beauty as a criterion of morals and art as the most expressive and generous pattern of life.

It was Aristotle who long ago fixed the most significant and pregnant meaning of art. He contrasted it with nature; it is artfulness or artifice; what man does to nature; it is what man does to a nature which was not made for him, but which he must accommodate himself to and subject to his own best uses. Bridging a river or broiling a steak are instances of art in its simplest and most rudimentary sense. All civilization is in essence an art; human intelligence applied to the conditions of nature, and human dreams turned through the technique of sciences and institutions into some-

thing like order and delight. If without government, as Hobbes insisted, life would be
'poor, nasty, brutish and short,' government is
only one of the arts by which the human animal has turned his instincts into beneficent
methods, and the chaos of his environment into
a tolerable order. The step from the bearable
to the beautiful is not very far. The fine arts
are simply those arts in which what is done is
done beautifully and for its own sweet sake.
The sheer unquestionable and unquestioned
joy of beholding a beautiful thing, and the liberating activity of producing it, have been regarded throughout recorded history as among
the clear and impeccable goods of life.

The call to art is thus not at all a call to
burial in a museum or stultification in a concert hall. It is merely a reminder that in the
ways of creation that we call art and in the objects we call beautiful are the instances of what
we might wish our lives and our society to be
continually like. Often before a still life we are
caught in a moment's act of vision that is instant and absolute peace. It is such serenity
as love and friendship at moments provide,
and which a more generous order of society
might make more continually possible. In lis-

tening to the ordered march, momentum, and disciplined passion that is Brahms's 'First Symphony,' we have a sense of what life, if its conditions were both more sensible and more spontaneous, might be like.

What troubles — and justly troubles — the critics about our civilization is not that people fail to buy books and pictures and talk the High Lingo of the nouveau art. What troubles them is that the sense for beauty and the demand for it are so notably absent and so little cultivated in our lives. What is needed is not so much new museums to bore more Philistines. What is demanded is a type of education and morale that will make beauty regarded as less of an effete stranger in our midst.

The artist knows that what gives his work and his life reality is individuality. He resents that standard mechanization of life that deprives lives of anything of a personal signature or character. Some years ago, Helen Marot suggested that we make room in industry for something she suggestively called the 'creative impulse.' Hilaire Belloc and G. K. Chesterton sentimentalize much about the days when each handicraftsman put his own individual and unique touch upon his own work which he saw through from its design to its finish. Perhaps that is impossible for a civilization committed to quantity and machine reproduction. But certainly there could be more room for freedom and individuality, in our teaching, our writing, and our ideas in a civilization that did not put a premium upon standardized things, patterns, and ideas in everything from collars to cantatas.

Art for Philistia should begin with something more fundamental than courses in art or provision for artistic training, though it is curious how completely, for the most part, our universities have made provision for everything but the imaginative life. It should be part of our education to train us to a sense of the æsthetic possibilities of acts and objects not commonly thought within the domain of art. It is part of our gospel of efficiency to have become careless of all the means and incidents in life that might become durably and pervasively beautiful. After a sojourn in England, the returning American is shocked by the extent to which speech with us has become simply a hard ugly method of gettings things said. And how easily the words and cadences of our language might turn the daily intercourse of our lives

into something itself possessing the quality of
an arresting delight! Perhaps, again, in a sub-
wayed and radioed and Fordized civilization,
courtesy and grace of manner in social relations
would appear too effete and eighteenth century
an importation. But the connection between
manners and morals is something more than
accidental; the form of doing and what is done,
like the form and content in music, are indissolubly wedded to each other. No civilization
can be lovely in attainments, the quality of
whose daily living is ugly.

In his latest volume of 'Impressions and
Comments' Havelock Ellis becomes almost
bitter in his denunciation of the extent to which
our civilization has wandered from the path of
beauty. He is forever contrasting a beautiful
moment in love, in the ecstasy of the dance, or
in the sight of sea gulls flying, with the tawdriness and horror of our architecture, our cities, and our social relations.

There is cause for bitterness, no doubt. But
cause, too, for hope. Never before since the
sunny freedom of the Greeks was there more
of a chance to have the attitude of the artist
and the ideals of art become the criteria and
centers of our lives. We are freed from many of

the outworn stupidities and hypocrisies. We know perfectly well that whatever divinity we dream, it is only our own artful intelligence that can convert it into the realities of our lives. The new morale, if it is to be at all, will be a universal art of life. Through such an art we may turn the turbid stream of living into something colorful, fluent, and free.

There are many forces making in the direction of treating life as a problem in art. Not the least of these is the habituation even of Philistia to the cadence, the clarity, and the serenity of beauty. Somewhere Plato speaks of life as a listening, a listening to a fine music whose intervals are too subtle for the casual and promiscuous ear. It is perhaps not too fantastic to suppose that the way in which music seems genuinely to have made its way in America, may augur well for the future sweetness and fluency of life on this continent. An imagination attuned to the beautiful precisions of music will not remain long patient with the major discords of life. The harmony of the musician may win us to the view of making something more of a harmony of our society and our lives. We may come to hate hate, condemn misunderstanding, and social inequalities, not because they are wrong but because they are ugly deformations on the face of our civilization.

There are signs even that painting, so long a stepchild in this country, and architecture, too, are coming into their own. There are beginning to be reared about us structures in steel and stone that will feed the eye and the imagination as well as house the worker and his work. There is, too, something wistful and hopeful in the way in which thousands stand rapt along the galleries of the Metropolitan Art Museum in New York, listening to music among the marbles. And there is hope also in the very discontent which torments the rebel against Main Street who misses the space and splendor of the Place de la Concorde and the imagination which made them possible.

It is hard to tell where the passion for beauty, once stimulated, may lead us. It may transform our ugly urban civilization into something more shapely, simple, and humane. Philistia, awakened to art, may cease to be Philistia. The critics of our civilization who are most effective are not the rebels, the cynics, and the satirists. They are those artists in writing, in thought and in sound and in color, who are bit by bit displaying to us the ingredients of a beautiful world. There is so much of vitality, energy, and freshness in our civilization that is amenable to forms of beauty that no artist will flee the challenge. The sense for beauty can be continually fed by artists too busy creating beautiful things to curse an ugly environment. Nor does this mean that we shall turn into a nation of æsthetes fleeing from reality to arabesques. It will mean simply that habituation to the beautiful in art will be retroactive upon our lives.

Schiller long ago wrote some beautiful essays on the æsthetic education of man. We are just beginning to learn that to cultivate the ear, the eye, and the imaginations of our children, to educate them to beauty, is one of the easiest and most persuasive ways to convert them to the good. If we educate the children of Philistia to beauty, to its enjoyment and to its making, the civilization of the future will not only contain more beautiful things, but life in it will be something nearer to the creation, the rhythm, the freedom and discipline that is art.

PATTERNS FOR THE FREE

'A POET,' says Thomas Love Peacock, 'is a semi-civilized barbarian in a civilized age. The march of his intellect is like that of a crab, backwards.' But even men of letters, so often the facile *ignoranti* of their generation, cannot remain long or altogether insensitive to the transformations in thought and in daily life which are making the contours of a new age. Poets breathe the common air; they cannot escape the poison of new ideas, though they may never have heard the name of the most deadly current bacillus. It was to be expected that the work of Darwin and Lyell should eventually find related imaginative utterance in a Hardy or an Anatole France. The laboratory finds its public voices among writers who have never seen a test tube. The new psychology affects novelists who could not identify an intelligence quotient or measure a reaction time.

In the same way it is inevitable that the rumble of industry should have reached even the Ivory Tower. The tumult of cities and the nervous anarchy of a jazz age must necessarily find appropriate voices and adequate patterns. Poets may yearn to move among eternities but the stream of their consciousness is colored with all the deposits of that life which most of them daily live in a mechanized, standardized and urbanized civilization.

The revolts against tradition in literature have too often been explained away as the mere exhibitionism of literary eccentrics or of writers perversely weary of beautiful classic moulds. The desire for change is far more plausibly explained by the rise of mechanical science, the spread of industry and the sophistication of psychology than by any merely personal foible of an abstract *littérateur*.

The revolt against traditional patterns in literature has been parallel with the revolt against traditional patterns in thought and life. In comparison with the revolution of our ideas concerning God and sex (the most cosmic and the most personal of human experiences), a modification of merely literary conventions may seem altogether trivial. What is a change in a cadence compared with a change in a creed? Mechanical inventions have changed the range and the intimate detail of the lives of most denizens of the planet. A verbal device of a novelist may hope at most to touch the imaginations of thousands; a chemist deals with poison gases that may kill or synthetic foods that may nourish millions. Why, one may well ask, should changes in the patterns of literature merit the attention of those interested in the larger and more serious patterns of our lives? Why should rhetoric become more important than existence?

If changes in literary forms were simply verbal and rhetorical, they would indeed be unimportant. But the revolts in the last fifty years have been expressions of those deeper and more pervasive changes which literature is gradually learning to express. There has been, in the first place, a reaction against the genteel tradition in literature. Writers have wearied of the routine prettiness of a 'literary' poetry. They have sickened of the stereotype beauties of a tepid, abstract and elegant world. Time and again in the history of literature the same phenomena have occurred. Writers who have wished to be something more than flutists in words have wanted to give expression to all the possible areas of human thought and emotion. It is precisely this concern with those larger tracts of experience that makes Shakespeare seem to most readers so immeasurably more massive than Racine's tutored rhetoric of his so beautiful, so restricted, and so rhetorical a world. Now the moderns, too, wish the scope of literature to be enlarged to permit the expression of that variety of thought and that anarchy of emotion which is coming to seem so peculiarly characteristic of our age. Poets have occasionally sought new forms and devices for their own sakes, and have found in a freshness of rhythm or a strange new trick of dialogue the sheer delight of an original technical beauty. In an imperfect universe any good is a cause for gratitude; and the searchers after novel loveliness ought to be thanked rather than forgiven. But, for the most part, the novelists and poets of the last twenty-five years have been feeling for and working toward new forms for more responsible reasons. They have found the old forms inadequate to express those miscellanies of life hitherto inadmissible to the literature of the genteel tradition.

The pursuit of new forms is thus engendered as part of the interest in a newer subject matter, and a larger one. Contemporary fiction, among its more serious practitioners, is no longer content with that prescribed and gardened terrain, cultivated so exquisitely and tactfully by an Edith Wharton and with such gravity by a Henry James. Their choice and smooth human landscapes now have come to seem meaningless elegant house parties on large enclosed estates shut in by tall trim hedges from the vulgar general life. The novelists, led by Bennett in England, by Lewis in America, have been reaching out among the rich areas of dulness and poverty, of humdrum tragedy and the dull edged comedy of the common man. They have passed from lawns in Surrey or terraces in Newport to the mean streets and mean souls of middle class life.

In the place of a poetry 'warbling,' as Norman Douglas somewhere says 'about buttercups,' we have a Masters in America, or a Masefield or a Wilfrid Gibson in England to try to make a music out of the glare and heat and routine of our own omnipresent industrial civilization. The polite blue surfaces of social romance have been ruffled by the uprush of dark passions not hitherto recognized as decent or tolerable materials for fiction. The actual unspoken torments of sex no longer lie veiled in the urbanities of a Howells or a Henry James. The net spiritual result of the recent serious movements in fiction may be suggested by saying that fiction has been bringing into its province whole areas of human concern that the older generation would have regarded as inelegant or unliterary. Writers as different as James Joyce and Sherwood Anderson have been attempting to bring literature, as Socrates brought philosophy, from the clouds to the haunts of men.

Underlying the appearance of new forms lies thus an interest in wider materials. Literature is no longer to be regarded as the expression of a choice and pretty, but of an authentic and comprehensive, cosmos. Dreiser brings the actualities of sex; Lewis brings the actualities of business; Anderson, D. H. Lawrence, James Joyce, and Virginia Woolf bring the misty and turbid recesses of the spirit into the field of literary subject matter. A wider area of the social scene is uncovered, and the novelist cuts deeper into the psychological soil. The outer aspect and the inner ferment have both been more completely and more minutely studied. It has come to seem a little tepid to be interested in writing merely as a subtle working in curious and irrelevant jewels. The adult artist is beginning to recognize that to write, if one is not merely to hum, is to write about something, and that writing is ultimately rendered great by the weight and poignancy of what it says and represents. Sinclair Lewis is impressive perhaps chiefly because he renders so bitterly and unmistakably the portrait of a futile civilization; Sherwood Anderson, because he follows so sincerely the inner stream of lost and reaching souls.

The interest in the enlargement of subject matter, if it has led to the search for new forms, has been partially eclipsed in interest by these forms. There are many reasons why an artist may come to be fascinated by new forms for their own sake. One of them arises from his awareness of a wider content than the older forms have embodied. The artist may feel that the formal rhythms and the stereotyped vocabulary of the older poetry, the objective and materialistic photography of fiction are inadequate to represent those wide tracts of experience and those fine *nuances* of feeling which are the business of a responsible modern intelligence. Or the interest in new forms may be the characteristic delight of the virtuoso in experiment, the abstracted pleasure of the technician in an unprecedented handling of words.

The arguments for experiments in verse forms are by this time familiar, and the experiments by this time dull. We have ceased to hear of late of the slavery of rhyme and the strait-jacket of the formal metres. We have tired a little of puny imitators of Whitman's roaring freedom. But the tinkling and the controversy have left a net deposit that is all to the health of English verse. The disciples of free verse wished to remove poetry from the character of a formal ballet at a court function. They wished it to be the spontaneous song of a democratic and miscellaneous world. They have been more spontaneous than singing, and they have often widened the area of poetic materials without making that material into music. But their intention was generous and their effect salutary. Now that the heat of rebellion has died down, we know that the revolt against standard forms has been a little silly. Milton uses a thousand forms of blank verse in a thousand lines, and in the hands of a master, even the jeered heroic couplet may become a singing of endless variety; rhyme may become a subtle and pliable instrument of iteration and psychological echo.

The net effect of the revolt in poetry has been to release poets from the conventions of the poetasters and render them free voices of whatever of passion and intelligence they are provoked to in their life in the contemporary world. It may be a generation yet before the atmosphere of the modern mind becomes sufficiently pervasive to touch even poets. It was several hundred years after naturalism started in Greece that Lucretius appeared in Rome to translate the science of a free spirit into music. But intelligence is becoming domestic in modern verse. Miss Millay treats love and E. A. Robinson treats failure and success with an unremitting ironic intelligence that is the very tincture of its time, and they sing in forms too beautiful to become dated. Other poets are learning from them that the free mind is not doomed to flee even beauty. All forms, the sonnet included, are free, so only that they are subdued to the articulate intention of an authentic emotion and an honest mind. An artist will find forms to fit his moods, and his moods may eventually be magnificent enough to match the wide canvas of possible human settings, and the subtilized organ of possible human passions. Only those enslaved to rebellion will say that free verse is the sole adequate instrument for a free poet. It is striking that Edwin Arlington Robinson, in many ways the most emancipated in temper and the most magnificent in reach of contemporary poets, has found in the ancient and austere pattern of the sonnet a suitable instrument for the singing of imaginative depths and freedom.

In the case of fiction there have been reasons far more serious than those of the virtuoso why new forms have been sought and found. James Joyce, more intelligibly and availably, Virginia Woolf, and, to some degree, May Sinclair have contrived to throw into suspicion the objective realism of Galsworthy, Bennett, and Wells. Their method in fiction is indirectly — in the case of May Sinclair, fairly directly — the fruit of the new psychology and of the more recent philosophies.

From the new psychology these writers and many others have learnt the cardinal fact, known though not formulated by the common man, that people's behavior is as much determined by the things they do not think about as by the things about which they consciously do think. From philosophies new and old they have learnt that what is 'really real' is what happens in, or to, a man's consciousness; that the objective world dissolves in fact and in analysis to what it is as experienced in the living stream that is a person's thought or emotion. D. H. Lawrence has tried and succeeded, despite all his turbid falterings, in making clear or at least phosphorescent what happens in the dark forest of the troubled subconscious self. James Joyce and Virginia Woolf have tried to reveal what the world is through and in the minds of those to whom it appears in broken flashes and intermingling echoes. The older method that revealed character in action and action in terms of doors and windows, tables and chairs, the meat, potatoes and furniture of our daily lives, has come to seem unconvincing. It has, moreover, come to seem irrelevant to those novelists and those readers interested in the most primary of all realities, a man's soul. The new psychological method in fiction (a method, by the way, as old as Chekhov and Dostoievsky) is not a mere playful variation in form. It amounts to little short of a revolution in the fictionist's approach to life and his conception of the content of narrative literature.

The way in which, as the psychologists say, we apperceive our world is largely a matter of habit. And we are certainly habituated to the older method in fiction. Even the receptive find James Joyce as difficult as he is impressive. Our minds, as Bergson long ago suggested, are geometrized. We see life in fixities, in the routine categories of mechanism and of logic.

The sane man, it has been said, holds a lunatic in leash. And that poignant madness that lies simmering in the interior of many lives, outwardly sensible and polite, is only now being uttered in its native idiom by writers like May Sinclair, Virginia Woolf, and James Joyce. That idiom of the basic hum and simmer of our lives, those glimpses of terrifying and real abysses, of haunting and ugly echoes, of thunderclaps of beauty arising suddenly in the midst of obscene reveries: these are surprising and terrible things. They fit into no usual codes and into no hitherto outspoken grammars of emotion. We are inclined to find them unintelligible or horrible or absurd. It will require many years of training to understand these new fluent languages by which novelists are trying to introduce us to the sobbing and staccato current of ourselves.

Dr. Johnson long ago pounded his walking stick testily on the pavement and thought that thus he had refuted Berkeley's conviction that the world was merely our ideas and perceptions. Many critics of these newer novelists bang, too, on the pavement or on their own heads and insist that these hard things alone are realities, and that only the stiff objective language and method of the older fiction is intelligible. The newer novelists are trying to find patterns that will free us to look keenly at ourselves. These patterns in fiction are not yet found. But these writers are pointing the way toward an art that will be as lucid and succinct and intelligible as the old, and will speak more eloquently and fully to man of his own unpetrified soul.

PHILOSOPHY FOR THE LAWLESS

THERE has been reported from colleges all over the country an increasing interest in the study of philosophy. Public forums and institutions of adult education find as responsive and eager attention to the wider questions of life and destiny as to specific discussions of the reform of judicial procedure or the short ballot. A distinguished foreign philosopher like Bertrand Russell comes to this country and fills a large auditorium to standing room with a question no more caught in the immediate tangle of current affairs than 'Life and Mechanism.' Even the daily lucubrations of Dr. Frank Crane and his fellow sermonizers in print are significant. These quotidian commentaries are, after a fashion, philosophy; they attempt to deal with ultimate questions for the ultimate and average consumer.

One wonders what the young intelligence of our time expects from a study that has from the days of ancient Athens been popularly dismissed as foolish or useless. Is it possible that metaphysics has come into its own? Is it

credible that the lay intelligence has discovered that 'philosophy is not harsh or crabbed as dull fools suppose'? What does the now notorious younger generation want of philosophy and what may it hope to find?

It appears to me that the fresh minds of our time are turning to philosophy in the hope of finding there the fruits of which the rebellions of this and previous younger generations have sown the seeds. They are seeking a synthesis out of all those atoms of insight or destruction which have characterized contemporary thought. They wish to piece together a mosaic of a faith by which they may live, out of those twin operations of the present intellectual spirit, discovery and disillusion. I believe they may out of contemporary thinking find such a synthesis. But what they wish and what they can find, may perhaps be better understood if we endeavor first to discover what it is of which they feel the lack, and what it is of which they have been robbed by the current disillusion.

The business of a younger generation has long been conceived to be that of rebellion. The middle aged, by tradition, insist on the sacredness of the accredited tables of the law;

the young are characteristically pictured in the operation of breaking them. But for us of this generation there is indeed very little rebellion left to do. From the break-up of the Middle Ages to the present, idol smashing has been a favorite occupation of the intelligent. In the last twenty-five years that exciting enterprise has been incredibly accelerated. From all sides the forces of criticism and attack have come. Their object has been every conceivable fixed tradition. The sources of disillusion have been many, and by this time the disillusion has become depressingly general. The human race, especially that young and energetic portion of it by which the world's work is kept going, has never been able to live without some faith, even if it were faith in a fiction. And we are, I think, beginning to note the turn toward a search for a saving and reconstructive wisdom. From disrespect for the old foolish laws, we are turning to look for some law of reason to regulate our lives.

It would, I believe, be difficult to find an educated and sensitive young mind of our day who has not passed through the tumult of most of the possible disillusions. Nearly a half century ago Matthew Arnold wrote about living

between two worlds, one dead and one powerless to be born. We are, half a century later,
still living between those two worlds, and the
number of things that are dead have been increased by the killing arts of irony and information. We are beginning to suspect that if the
process of assassination goes on much further,
we may be killing our own souls. In killing our
faiths we are killing ourselves. For it is in its
living faiths that the life of the spirit consists.

The central moving faith that has for most
young minds collapsed is, broadly speaking,
religion. In the late nineteenth century it was
evolution and physics that made theology impossible. With the maturing youth of our day
it is anthropology and Anatole France. It is no
longer so much questions of the existence and
goodness of God that worry the skeptic; he is
fretted by the ironies and contradictions of his
own mind. Frazer in 'The Golden Bough,'
Lévy-Bruhl in 'Primitive Mentality,' George
Foot Moore in 'The Birth and Growth of Religion,' to mention only a few, have revealed to
us some horrifying analogies. One cannot resist an ironic comparison between our noblest
ceremonies and the bloodiest of primitive ritu-

als, between our holiest mysteries and the grossest of savage superstitions. No informed mind and sensitive spirit can go through even a modicum of anthropological literature without having this corruption of comparative irony eat into his faith. Whatever reconciliations the skeptic makes for himself between religion and science, whatever wistful hold he makes on the nobilities and idealisms enshrined in traditional religion, he can no longer take that tradition literally. He has passed from naïveté to criticism, and if he returns to belief it will be as a critical believer.

It required, perhaps, only this central faith to go, for all those minor faiths by which men live to follow. Religion which, as Henry Adams saw it, was the keystone in the arch of mediæval life, remained so, many centuries afterward, in the emotions of men. And when one begins to be skeptical about the cosmos, skepticism in other fields is easy. In moral questions, it does not take long for the young to make pertinent and terrible interrogations. It is indeed easier to check up in experience codes of expected moral action than to check up on the attributes of God. God is, after all, in His heaven, but the traditional moral standards and their fruits can be observed here upon earth.

The young mind, resolute and free, does not take long to realize that many of the traditional moral standards are fixed catchwords and labels by which the spontaneous impulses of human beings are molded to the expected social tradition. It is not for nothing that the anthropologists have shown how similar are the prohibitions and approvals of our own society to those cruel compulsive rituals and taboos by which primitive man was regimented into the traditions of his tribe. The old fixities in the relationship of the sexes, of the family and of the social classes, property and the accustomed proprieties, have all come into question. It has become clearer and clearer that the acceptance of many of these rises not from reason in theory or splendor in practice, but from the squalid fears and compulsions of the tribe. Respect for many of the current taboos or commendations seems to the young emancipated to place them in a class with the cave man and the gorilla. There has been a reversion from high words to the festering rottenness which exalted gospel faintly covers and perfumes. The young freeman looks every gift horse in the mouth, including those of tradition, which the middle-aged, the most contemporary of our ancestors, have brought to us down the stream of time.

What holds true of morals holds true likewise of that field of social and political action in which, after all, moral distinctions are tried out and made effectual. How painfully naïve seems that faith in humanity and humanity's reform by itself, shared with a clear and noble fervor by such giants as Comte and John Stuart Mill. A humanity whose intelligence is rotted by its own inner darknesses and blindnesses! How can we out of poor bundles of chaos expect clarity and light? Psychoanalysis has almost revived a doctrine of original sin. The devils that lie in the dark heart of each of us will hardly generate an angelic society.

And if we are naïve enough to expect it, one look at the outer political scene is enough to discourage the most hearty. In peace, patriotism is turned into sinister propaganda, and nationalism into the red badges of international horror. War, once the synonym for a flaming idealism, has become with such bitter obviousness the brutal mechanical expression of vast

163

political and economic forces which no glimmer of faith or idealism can control.

In disillusion with the practical scene, the mind of our generation has turned to the arts. There, too, it has found itself in a quagmire of uncertainties, skepticisms, and depressions. It has seen the life, grandeur, and exaltation once held to be the peculiar gift of art, denounced as false, romantic and absurd. It has read in the new school of biographers that all idols have clay feet. It has seen the art of literature degenerating into a study of clay feet. Our novels have turned from the soft sublimities of Tennysonian love to enshrining the root of lust; for Platonic rapture has been substituted protoplasmic thrills. The very absurdity of the comparison between James Joyce's and Tennyson's 'Ulysses' accents the change. The towering images of physical passion have replaced

> For I sail beyond the sunset and the baths
> Of all the Western stars until I die.

In music, for the clear sonorities of the great tradition there are the broken rhythms, the wild cacophonies, the strained harmonies by which artists in sound have tried to utter the passionate disintegration of the modern spirit. In painting, for the serenities of classic composition we have the fevered, highly colored attempts to communicate, through a superficial formlessness, a deep sense of significant form.

Possibly no one, not an academic idiot, has failed to see the value of all these rebellions and disintegrations. The fixed musty world has been shaken up. Vivacity and a sense for change have become the dominant notes in our thinking and our life. We have come to hate, before all else, the formal and dead. We have moved into what James calls an open universe. If there is less security than in the tight world of tradition, there is more adventure; if there is less verbal nobility, there is much more intimacy and spontaneity. Above all we are living in a free world, freed of dogma in religion, of fixity in morals, of the academic in art and the formal in manners. Nobody wants to move back into the snug confines of the Victorian world again. We are free. But what price freedom?

There is a well-known Russian story by Chekhov, I think, of a man whose wife had run away, whose finances were ruined, whose house had burned down, and who was, in conse-

quence, explicably unhappy. It was the deep
of winter. He took a sleigh and went driving
off into the cold, with the sleigh bells merrily
jingling. He was free to go where he pleased,
and he did not know or consider where he was
going.

I think this is the situation of the young
minds of our time. They are beginning to feel
lost and drifting in a world out of which, along
with many shoddy old fixities and lies, they
have seen many lovely myths and inspiring
dreams destroyed. If they have been freed
from the old arbitrary laws, they have found
no new reassuring sanity or counsel. If they
have exploded factitious idealisms, they have
no new sound ones. If they no longer have
galling commands to obey, they have no clean
and urgent programme to follow.

What they are hunting for in philosophy, if
I mistake not, is something like a law, a law
not in the sense of a command but of a guide
to action. If the old order is gone irrevocably,
they do not, therefore, relish chaos. What
kind of order can they project for themselves
on the basis of a frank and unhypocritical feeling of the world?

In the first place, if they listen to the voice of

contemporary scientific thought, they will find that it is possible to have an idealism without unction or tears or false beliefs. Much of the paralysis of disillusion, so cuttingly expressed by Aldous Huxley in 'Antic Hay,' comes from those colors of chaos and meanness in which many contemporary writers have essayed to paint the truth about nature and life. Much of the cynicism is, as is usual in such cases, the outlet for a piqued and defeated idealism.

Suppose we accept the contributions of recent science as to the mechanical conditions and the animal basis of life. The miracle of the spirit that protoplasm generates and matter nourishes is not rendered any the less varied, singing or wonderful. To say that it is, would be like saying that the serene majesty of César Franck's D Minor Symphony is not there because the music is played by a hundred mediocre looking human animals, scraping strings, blowing wooden reeds, and beating skins. The contemporary mind, so recently habituated to looking matter and the natural world full in the face, has never been able to believe anything but vulgarity of matter. It has failed to remember or to observe what living and beautiful incarnations matter can take, and to what wingedness and music of the spirit it can rise. It has become a stock trick of artists in modern despair to paint a stark picture of the bleak mechanical world, where, 'blind to good and evil, impotent matter rolls on its relentless way.' But in that crass mechanism how lovely are the sunsets, and in these fated short cycles of birth and decay how much of deathless wonder and beauty comes to fulfillment. If man lives in slime — and there is slime always at the core of the soul — it is nevertheless this briefly animated dust that beholds stars, writes symphonies, and imagines God. The rebellious modern mind is very like those *révoltés* from the drabness of middle western towns, whose constant theme is bitterness and denunciation. We need, perhaps, most of all to become naturalized in the natural world. To describe or to face experience in terms only of its physical and animal machinery is no more complete or relevant than it would be to describe a charming dinner party by talking exclusively about the digestive processes of the guests.

The loss of a literal belief in an eternal personal God and a traditional salvation has its compensating side. We may come to appreciate with more freedom and completeness those reaches toward perfection which the great religions have with such infinite tenderness and poetry enshrined. We may substitute for a mumbled lip service toward a God who is merely a name and a household habit, a piety toward that cosmos which has generated so many gracious things, flowers and friends, our hunger for immortality, our myths of heaven, and our dreams of God.

We may thus become reconciled to the natural world, to the irreducible brutality of matter and the undeniably basic animality of life. We may even come to cherish them for the spirit which they generate and the beauties they subserve. It is possible, in the same spirit, to face moral problems, without being a fool, a sentimentalist, or a prig. Ethics has so long been associated with sourness and stultification, with curates, with old maids and college professors, that the free mind has fled from any discourse savoring of morals. It suggests too much of that unction and pharisaism of which the world has for ages been wrenching itself free.

The new paganism sees life, as the ancient paganism saw it, a bright interval between two endless deaths. It asks only to be let alone to crowd that pulsing interval with happiness. Why listen to the chilling voice of superstition calling itself duty when there is so little time in which to enjoy so much? But even the free man has found himself tormented by two conflicting impulses or through living with others whose interests collided with his own. In experience some choices are forced upon us, some rejections must be made. And it requires not the preaching of a moralist but the unmistakable nature of things to show us that absolute liberty is impossible. We may resent the false, outworn, and unnecessary repressions that parents and teachers have forced upon us. But some order or organization of life is indispensable if we are to live at all or to live at all happily. Absolute liberty would be absolute insanity. It is found chiefly in asylums, where hysterical patients afford the most striking example of people who have let themselves go. It is ours to find the most fruitful and generous forms of life. We must make for ourselves a discipline, not one that is suggested to us by a cruel or a fanatical moralist, but one arising out of the inescapable conditions of nature and of life.

The problems of morals do not cease because

we have thrown overboard the old pretended solutions that did not solve. Precisely because the new generation has been freed from much killing cant and narrowness and superstition, its mind is clear and direct. It could do much to clarify the human scene, and give sweeter and fairer perspectives to the common life. All that is required is patience, inquiry, and good will. There is little time to waste in hitting at past errors, considering the vastness and variety of the business in hand. If our current practices, our industry, our commerce, our education are primitive and cruel, they might be civilized and humanized by those same alert intelligences that now satirize or turn their backs on them altogether. If psychoanalysis has taught us more than we ever knew or dared to acknowledge about the dark and sinister corners of our hearts, so much the more information have we toward the cleansing of our spirits and the ordering of our lives. If we know till it hurts what is wrong with the American scene, its standardizations, rush, brutality, and dulness, it is ours to change them, as God says to Peter in H. G. Wells's novel.

The latter-day pagan knows more or less what he misses in the current turmoil and chaos. The word 'beauty,' used for so many different festivals of the spirit, perhaps best describes that vividness and clarity which the contemporary marketplace does not reveal. So the pagan flees, as of old, to the ivory tower. He finds there, too often, simply a morose photography of the chaos from which he has fled, or a thin æsthetic tickling of the palate provided for him by such men as Huxley and Van Vechten, artists in phosphorescent decay. The arts used to be shores of eternity upon which we might rest from our voyages in the restless deeps of time. Too largely now they have become satirical reporting, as in Sinclair Lewis, or sickly exquisiteness and meaningless embroidery, like the poetry in the little reviews. The young disillusionists need a new Saint Thomas to write them a new 'Summa Theologica.' All the parts of human experience in the grand mediæval synthesis fitted snugly into that universe whose comforting principle was a living God. The painter painted, the builder builded, even the juggler, as in the famous legend of the juggler monk, juggled for the glory of God, or of the Virgin. Can we hope for a reconstructive faith, rising out of the picture of the world that science and sophistication reveal for our belief? I believe we can.

Such men as William James, Dewey, Santayana, have made the outlines of that picture for our generation. Nature and life are at bottom, if you will, meaningless, blind, and chaotic. But they are malleable to an intelligence that faces them with candor and courage. Out of this miscellaneous soil of things, something like a garden may be made. But weeds must be removed; growths must be tended. And we must know how to distinguish between flowers and weeds.

Every artist and every athlete knows how stern a regimen is imposed by an ideal. A harmony, among other things, means the exclusion of irrelevant noises. No tautness or swiftness is possible in the body without some denial of appetite or indulgent caprice. If we wish to make of our lives a clear and fluent music there is much that we must gird ourselves to, and much that we shall have to renounce.

'A marble temple shining on a hill.' That has been a favorite image of the sunlit pagan world. What shall be the image of our newer paganism? Music, perhaps, for our life and habits are in our day so caught in the flux of time. If the themes of our life are to flow with gathering clarity and splendor, we shall look to our instruments and to our playing. One wild note will stop or cloud the music; we must be disciplined craftsmen if our lives are to sound that harmony of which we dream. Our hands must be steady, and our senses sure, our action intelligent and our vision direct. We shall then seek a religion that utters our loyalty to the things of the spirit, a morality that is a programme toward a harmony of life, an art that is a clear picture of those eternities for which men can clearly continue to care.

REASON FOR THE RAPTUROUS

IT might appear that, when intellectualism, even among young men, has become an habitual disease, it were hardly necessary to write a defense of reason as a habit of life. But there are signs all over Europe and America of a growing revolt against reason. It may not, therefore, be without point to say something in defense of the cool reflective tradition. In Italy, for example, the younger philosophical men of letters seem preoccupied with a neo-mystical movement directed at once against the intellectualized idealism of the nineteenth century and the materialistic cynicism of the twentieth. In England, championed not least by the energetic though gloomy Dean, the right to be mystical is once more being urged. The subtlest of logics is being invoked in the campaign against the domination of life by thought. The cult of reason has had its fruits in cynicism, pessimism, and despair. The flowers of clear thought have not been altogether beautiful. From many unhappy quarters, therefore, the rebound has come. Too much mind, it is feared, has thinned the blood; the wanton use of logic has despoiled loveliness. Hence in literary criticism and programmes has come a demand, *vide* Croce or Sherwood Anderson, for less polish and more fire; in politics, *vide* Mussolini, energy is acclaimed as superior to counsel or compromise; in religion, *vide* Dean Inge or Mary Austin, mystical rapture has been sought in place of the intellectual love or the intellectual questioning of God.

To these revoltees, reason needs not so much an exposition as it needs an apology. They point out with justice that life becomes most alive and certainly becomes most completely justified in its high unexamined moments of completion. There are instants in friendship and in art when one is incited not to inquire but to enjoy. At such moments the mere fact of being is the experience of perfection. At such *crescendi* in otherwise routine days one resents the prying presence of reflection. For what is reason but the uninvited, unwanted guest at the festival of happiness? What does it do but shadow the so vivid present reality with suggestions of its precarious endurance, its high costs, or its wormy consequences? Those whom love has once taken to a height, or whom sensibility to line or color or sound has once quickened to a swifter awareness, may come to identify reflection with a lowering of vitality or a clipping of the spirit's wings.

From the Greeks down, there have been the now familiar prudential arguments for leading the life of reason. By many different philosophers in many different languages, the race has been informed that it pays to be prudent. One swallow, says Aristotle sententiously, does not make a summer. And the whole burden of the typical cautious moralist is that one glamorous impulse may ruin a life; one touch of flame may be the immolation of a career. The nonchalant way in which the race has ignored moral theory is proof enough of how futile such exhortations must be. It is no use telling a creature thirsty for joys that his body will not let him question, that he may, by refusing them, live joylessly forever. The moralists themselves have not appeared to deny that beyond the golden mean lay joys of still rarer metal. But traffic with such exotic goods has always seemed to them fraught with danger. Indeed the golden mean has been recommended chiefly, not because it was golden, but because it was safe. Half a life, the implication has been, is better than none. But it is no use calling human beings from a dangerous bliss to dull safety. Reason will win its votaries when the life of reason is shown, not to be safe, but to be even more seductive than the life of passionate impulse itself.

All arguments about the conduct of life are *a posteriori*. It is a familiar fact that it is not theory but temperament that determines our ultimate choices. But there is one plea for the reflective life that has not been sufficiently stressed and one, incidentally, that should appeal particularly to those avid of ecstasy. That consideration is the truth attested to by great lovers throughout history, that to any experience in art or in life, reason gives poignancy, volume, and depth. It is the light which intensifies the hues of all varieties of joy; it is the ray which penetrates to the deep heart of otherwise unknown and unknowable pleasures. No love becomes less vivid because the lover realizes consciously and completely the lineaments, the destiny, the budlike excellences, the weed-like weaknesses, of his beloved. The edge and dram of his passion lose nothing in force and gain much in tenderness because he knows the animal roots out of which his love has grown, or the dusty extinction to which he and his beloved and all their little fire are doomed. No connoisseur's pleasure is infected because his eye has been subtly trained to observe the particular niceties of line and color to which he has hitherto responded with a vague and leaping heart. There is no diminishing of joy to the musician because he has discovered in music an intricate, exciting pattern to be followed, not an opiate to be drunk swooningly. Nor finally, on a wider scale, is the lover of God less filled with Godhead because his disciplined mind has become a clear mirror of divinity. 'The heart,' said Pascal, 'has its reasons that reason does not know.' And it may be said, on the other hand, that reason has its joys that the heart alone could never find or fathom.

The illusion that the practice of understanding mitigates the experience of pleasure has several obvious sources. It is beyond doubt true that reason robs human beings of certain types and qualities of enjoyment that do not go with a clear head. Sentimentalism in love and superstition in religion, the rhetorical in literature and the gaudy in painting, are made forever impossible to those whose imaginations have been tempered by reflection. One is spoiled for affection without the saving salt of irony, and for romance without the antiseptic of common sense. Music without structure and poetry without substance are increasingly distasteful to those who come to all arts and to all experiences with their minds as well as their diaphragms. Intelligence beyond peradventure robs the human animal of his cheaper and more obvious pleasures. Even when in the grip of lust he cannot refrain from noting the brutal compulsion that thus constrains him to joy. Even when, incited by the flesh, his imagination carries him to mystical peaks of the spirit, he cannot help remembering the physical mechanisms that are the cause of his rare, unearthly dreams.

The amateur in the life of reason is necessarily self-conscious. For a while he distrusts his emotions altogether or enjoys them with a mental reservation of ennui or disdain. There are students of harmony and counterpoint, the intellectual amateurs of music, who will not admit to themselves that they are ever caught up by a swelling movement or an engulfing crescendo of sound. There are lovers, newly sophisticated with reason, who would not admit, even in mutual intimacy, that they have become for each other each other's universe. Thus to confess what is emotionally true, would appear to them intellectually silly. It is not reason that kills naïve joys and corrupts honest emotions. It is the self-consciousness that comes to those who have only lately learned to practice reason, or have not learned to practice it often.

Those in whom intelligent awareness has become a fixed mental habit know that that joy does not kill but rather sharpens rapture. The trained music lover knows that music has become for him an infinitely more various and extensive continent since he learned to move with ease from its pretty coast through its lovelier inland forests of harmony. The enchantment that once vaguely stirred his nerves now satisfies his acutely awakened sense and absorbs his aware and possessed mind. In addition to the merely emotional disturbance that music has been for him always, it now becomes an 'audible mathematics,' a logic piquantly sensuous in its medium and its appeal. It has turned into a song for the mind.

Nor does all this mean that he has lost the simpler vital pleasures of music. The tremble of a note, the movement of a melody, engage his senses more keenly even than they did of old, now that he has learned to study and to follow them more minutely. But he has acquired a new perspective, and his pleasure has a new dimension. Notes have become moments in the magnificent drama of sound. And, through the intercession of mind, he is enabled now to recognize past harmonies and recognize their emergence in strange new colors and in ultimate happy concords. The Bach 'Passacaglia,' from being a vast boring blur, has been transformed into a flawless, overwhelming pattern. The listener has acquired a possibility of musical pleasure far more intense and far more unearthly than the musical sensualist or the musical sentimentalist alone could ever know.

What is true of the enjoyment of music is true of the enjoyment of any art. To perceive with precision and with perspective — and that is what intelligent connoisseurship consists in — is to turn a merely brute excitement into a perduring spiritual delight. To have seen and heard and enjoyed with intelligence is not simply to have breathed an experience more deeply; it is to have conserved it long after it is over. The mere act of reflection, as those best know to whom it has become habitual, may become on occasion the most exquisite *volupté*. Especially when the subject matter of one's reflection is beautiful, like choice sensations of color or sound, to think is to become for a moment a sensorium of pure delight, a purified register of beauty. And what has once been caught in the eternal relations of thought may be called up as a recurrent shining memory when the first happy contact is over.

There will be those ready enough to admit that the pleasures of appreciation may be heightened when they are clarified and discriminated in reflection. A few will be ready to take on faith that the act of thought may itself be the most delicious of sensations. (Aristotle could conceive of no purer bliss for God.) But these same voices will be raised to protest that in the arts, on the productive side, no good can ever come from reflection. There have been dozens since Plato who have insisted that great artistic creation comes from a divine madness. And in our day, writers as far apart as Croce and Mary Austin have insinuated that in creation the sane are more than probably the mediocre. Certainly the highest achievements in art do seem to have sprung from something deep, primitive, and subconscious, dictated by an inner dæmon, a divine whispering voice. Metaphorically, at least, one is ready to accept the notion of some genius of a place or art speaking softly and with authority into the ear of a great artist. Even the layman is ready with his facile distinction between genius and talent.

Croce, who has been quoted by many more critics than have read him, did in all his labored 'Estetica' manage to make one point clear. It is the artist's intuition, not his technique, that matters. Line and color in painting, rhyme and rhythm in poetry, harmony and counterpoint in music, these do not signify much, if anything. The great and essential fact is what an artist feels, the acute center of his sincerity and rapture. The rest is machinery. Tolstoy went so far indeed as to insist that all that preoccupied the sophisticated critics, the devices and subtleties by which effects were produced, was so much testimony to the falsity and emptiness of contemporary art. Only the passionate image in an artist's soul was of importance. His gift was his vision of the truth; his art, in so far as it was art and not artifice, was his version of truth. And his version was as successful as his vision was sincere.

Croce and Tolstoy were both emphasizing something fundamental and just. Of that there can scarcely be a doubt in the mind of any one who has come suddenly into surprised contact with a masterpiece in any art. Pass along a gallery of pictures at any exhibition — canvas after canvas with all the certificated competence of the schools. There is no flaw of composition and no colored outrage upon the eye. All is effective and disciplined and dull. Then there meets the eye something whose impressive quality outruns definition and analysis. It seems the product of something other than competence; it is addressed to something more deep and private and authoritative than reason. The voice is the voice of genius and the language is that of unmistakable perfection. The picture appears to be more than an adroitly contrived *thing*: it is the visible sign of a passionate spirit, and in our own spirit it quickens passions below the precise formulas of the connoisseur.

It is the extraordinary difference between first and second rate in art that places them in two different worlds. In the case of first rate art, one cannot believe that what is so transcendent of analysis can possibly have been produced by mind. And in the case of second rate art, it is apparent always that the most competent academician absents himself from the felicity which is the signature of genius.

But certain corruptive illusions follow in the train of that recognition of the chasm between genius and talent. The genius that is absolute felicity is certainly a very different matter from the modest talent that wishes to substitute a vague intensity for discipline. No amount of intelligence will ever be a surrogate for the authentic fire. But a very good case may be made out from contemporary or historical examples for the contention that intelligence is the least neglected instrument which genius has used. What may genius be, indeed, but intelligence preternaturally felicitous and swift? Because a masterpiece keeps the secret of its production, it does not follow that it was produced without method at all. It is the little yearners after greatness, not the great, who counsel a slovenly dependence upon inspiration.

The living breath of a work of art is certainly the artist's vision, his sense of some phase of experience in which his quickened spirit has lived in fact or in imagination. The aim of art, it may be said, is to communicate that quickened sense to the observer. But the means of communication are always material means, just those strokes of the brush, just that arrangement of notes, just that collocation of chords. It requires training, precision, and the skill of the craftsman to translate a vague intense vision into a work of art. And it requires the connivance of mind on the part of the observer for the vision to become his as well as the artist's.

No creator ever killed a conception, some beauty in embryo, because of a sure technique. He merely communicated it the better. No observer was ever purloined of pleasure because he had trained eyes with which to see precisely, ears with which to hear exactly, and an intelligence with which to understand. All jewels gleam more beautifully in a clear intense light. All the facets of pleasure become more crystalline in the impeccable light of mind. The purest ecstasy may indeed be what the Hindu philosophers have claimed it to be, not the flight from but the closest embracing of thought.

In the conclusion of Shaw's 'Back to Methuselah,' in the section called 'As Far As
Thought Can Reach,' Shaw represents, it will
be remembered, a group of ancients. They are
gray people, these, who have passed beyond
the seduction of sense and the playtime of art
to the sober satisfactions of contemplation.
The picture of these intellectuals is not rapturous. The better image is, perhaps, Dante's.
Dante, conducted by Beatrice, has passed
through circle after circle of Paradise, and
through session after session of dialectical discussion with various learned saints. The bea-
tific vision in which he is lost at the end, the
fusion of instantaneous and eternal love and
light, these form the terminus of an intense
logical journey. Thought, too, may lead to the
divine rapture. Perhaps on the whole there is
no easier way.

SENTIMENT FOR THE CYNICAL

THERE is good reason why one finds so much interest — or affectation of interest — in the eighteenth century. That age of cool dry light and clear dry skepticism suits exactly the temper of the contemporary mind. The objects of our skepticism have changed, to be sure. We are no longer concerned with doubting God or miracles. We have come far beyond that to the stage where we doubt our friends, our heroes, and ourselves. Gibbon could doubt the authority of 'the three divine witnesses,' and bring down upon his undisturbed self a storm of theological abuse. We doubt the divine witness of our own best feelings, question the validity of our most persuasive ideals, and impugn the sincerity of those who profess or propagate them. And our latter-day skepticism provokes not even the compliment of dissent, much less that of abuse.

It is easy enough to understand the cynical temper with which we approach all contemporary questions and question all contemporary motives. We are reacting, in the first place, against the bric-a-brac and black walnut sentimentalism of the Victorians, much as Fielding's robust good sense reacted against the rhetorical virtues of Richardson and the rest. We are rebounding against the easy secular optimism of the pre-war period much as Voltaire rebelled against the easy theological optimism current in his time. Only with us it is not simple good health or good spirits that drive us to be honest in examining ourselves and our world. It is rather exacerbated nerves and unhappy sophistication. We have observed too nearly during the war and post-war years to what a mess high clean words and low soiled actions could bring the map of Europe and the map of life. We have come to prefer the pain of honest surgery to the perilous narcotics of sentimental delusion.

Our realistic temper has been nourished, as it may indeed have been produced, by the new technique the psychologists have given us for looking at ourselves. Chief among these has been what may broadly be called 'the new psychology.' Much of it, especially in its easy popular forms, may be unsound; not a little of it may be positively false and pernicious. But in its emphasis on the physiological basis of many of our moods and hopes, it has rendered forever impossible silly exaltation and unsubstantial rhetoric about ourselves. One cannot read or write a love lyric now without a little self-consciousness about glands and hormones. The highest reaches of emotion have their obscene little obbligati of awareness. Thoughts of God become juxtaposed with thoughts of sex, and even the common reader knows a lot about the seamy side of ecstasy.

It is perhaps good that this should be so. No mere mania can be passed off any longer as religious rapture, and no mere physiological excitement can parade as romance. We may borrow the language of the angels, but we have been taught to recognize our kinship to the apes. It has freed us of much nonsense about nobility, and has made possible a literature without tears.

But from other quarters have come even more serious instruments of doubt. The new 'intimate' schools of biography and history have made us hesitate to take any one, even if he be of the alleged great ones of the earth, more seriously than we take ourselves or our friends. The great marble statues of the heroic tradition have been badly weatherbeaten by

191

the salt winds of contemporary inquiry. Great generals become cowards in uniform, and great statesmen backstairs politicians on parade. There is an almost ghoulish glee in the way in which the new biographers have been making for us the discovery that the greatness we admired is nothing but a mirage made by time. Reverence is one of the emotions most conscientiously avoided by the hard new historians. Thus we have a life of Shelley in which we are shown, not the poet who soars like his own Skylark, but an amusingly foolish little adolescent who might have been a thousand other fools as well as Shelley. We are asked to remember, not the Wordsworth who gave us 'the light that never was on sea or land, the consecration, and the poet's dream,' but the Wordsworth who when old was dull and testy, and when young became the father of an illegitimate child. We are reminded, not of a Washington who after all did lead a Revolution and found a country — and that our own — but of a petty English squire by accident dining and gambling and swearing in Virginia instead of Surrey.

Nor is it only the great ones of the distant past about whom we have been receiving inside information until it hurts. There were those nearer great ones in the gullible days only recently past who seemed to illustrate the principle that a divinity might touch a man even if he happened to be alive and to be one of ours. It is a persistent romanticist who can still keep his idols of ten years ago in the face of the flood of 'frank' memoirs that have risen since the war.

But perhaps most devastating of all to our credulities is the recent withering analysis of our traditional virtues. Love of country? Any schoolboy reared on the newer history textbooks knows in what capitalistic quarters that useful instrument of imperialism has been manufactured. Family devotion? One smiles a little sadly at that. How many novels one seems to remember reading of late where family love was a killing clannishness kept up in the interests of a selfish father or mother or son. Friendship? The callow rhetoric of adolescence or the mutual endurance of people thrown inevitably into one another's society. Or of late there has been added the dark whisper of some incipient sexual perversion that lies behind any uncommon display of affection. Local pride, sentiment for places or things, excitement before pictures or poems, humility before age or kindling before youth — one voices these emotions at one's peril in the neighborhood of the contemporary satirist or in the awareness of one's own mind. The neurologist is called in to deal with cases of nobility, and sweetness will be greeted with a snicker.

Of course, on acquaintance, many of the professional cynics become, though it would turn their stomachs to be told so, quite dear people. They exemplify all the virtues which they professionally detest. They are — and Lord how they hate to admit it — good citizens, good lovers, good sons, and good friends. Their heads may be filled with all the antiseptics of modern knowledge; they persist in keeping that outmoded organ once known as the human heart. Those hearts are what one would once unashamedly have called good. Their own lives are often sufficient illustration of the fact that the sentiments they deride with such gusto continue to function in the world.

It might be the part of honesty and precision to face the actuality of these sentiments as part of a well-furnished realism. Talk as much as one pleases of hormones, people continue to fall in love and love continues for the nonce to transfigure their faces and their worlds. Bring on all the statistics of imperialism, and the sentiment of nationalism remains a fact, often a beautiful and stirring one, very like love indeed in its beauty and its possible disaster. The Rupert Brookes continue to love their England and sing of their love; the peasants of France persist in cherishing that corner of earth which is their life. Even cynics still found families, and love their parents and their sons. They recall with reluctant delight domestic foyers they have known that in their charm and mutual generosity and tolerance seemed indefeasible goods of a very dubious planet. The wise ones know that friendship is for profit; the scientists suspect its physical basis. Yet that conspiracy of vision and identity of mood in which friendship consists, continues to delude men. Friendship remains a naïve type of human satisfaction, an alliance at once intimate and free.

Now all these sentimental attachments may be foolish or they may be sinister. But they exist. They may be cruel and dangerous but they are compulsive. Any philosophy of life that leaves them out of account is as romantically distant from the facts as though it were bathed in sentimentality. For surely one of the worst forms of sentimentality is the denial of the operative power of sentiments in the economy of mankind.

Not but that one might wish that sentiment in human relations played a much less conspicuous rôle. Wars might certainly become less imminent if the sentiment of nationalism were less influential a fact. Lives might be serener, as Lucretius long ago bitterly insisted, if men were freed from the cancer of love. It is conceivable, too, from the standpoint of a truly adult humanity, that a life lived on the plane of pure intelligence might be altogether subtler and incomparably more steady in its joy. A race of passionless minds might in its cool and transparent unconcern move clearly among eternal issues, and survey untarnishable goods. Experience might become a pure mathematics; as clear and conclusive as a syllogism. From that high untroubled altitude how hysterical might seem all our little excitements, how childish our hopes and trivial our oscillating passions.

Thoreau says somewhere, what a pity it is that water however sweet turns putrid, but frozen it remains forever. Certainly it might be better if men were cool blocks of ice, forever frozen and forever pure. Society would be the free relationship of minds in logical play with each other. One would be free from all those little perturbations of spirit that make one long for an absent lover or friend. One companion would do as well as another or none would do equally well, since one would have the constant cold companionship of one's own thoughts.

It is the metaphysician's dream of a society of pure intelligence that lies behind some of the contemporary contempt for emotion. Perhaps only those who, like philosophers, have moved by habit in that realm know what its austere pleasures are. For the passion for detachment is itself a passion, though a rare one, and the adventure of thought a true adventure though open to few.

But there is a more general human argument against susceptibility to promiscuous emotion. It is the grown man's distaste for hysteria or sloppiness. Like the rationalists of the eighteenth century we have come to dread all forms of that sentimentalism that used in the eighteenth century to be dismissed as 'enthusiasm.'

It is not that we wish to deny or to abolish emotion. We resent its waste, its excess, or its imitation. The most passionate music is not the most luscious; a great violinist scorns the tremolo. Beethoven speaks more quietly but no less intensely than Tschaikowsky; pathos is not limited to symphonies labeled 'Pathétique.' The classic lyrics are chiseled understatements of emotion.

'I loved you, Athos, once, long ago,' wrote Sappho, and the feeling in that simple declarative is not diminished or lost in a sea of sentimental exposition. The contemporary mind, sick of all the lush bravura of emotion, has conceived an ideal of tempered control.

But to control passion, there must be passion to control. If silent men are strong, it is on the supposition that they might say something if they would. And passion under discipline is widely different from the highly romantic dream of a passionless world.

There are already signs of a revolt against the new puritanism which confuses aridity with strength and anæmia with power. There is a growing recognition even among scientists of the reality of that world of sentiments among which most human beings have their most vivid lives.

The sentiments of man are, after all, older and deeper than his reason. The 'really real' elements of a man's world are those features of his experience realized in the intimacy of emotion. Descartes wished to found a philosophy solely on 'clear and distinct ideas.' But it may well be, in the light of modern knowledge, that ideas are not the basic materials out of which to construct a philosophy. The world that we know through our intelligence is woven out of the most tenuous and most secondary of abstractions. The color of a sunset or the voice of a friend is metaphysically more real than the structure of atoms or the velocity of light. The first are individual, concrete, and alive; the second are skeletal generalities. All that our minds can give us is a dead abstraction of what comes to us in the tang and pressure of a given moment. What we call emotions or what we dismiss as sentiments is simply inward awareness of the most intensely real outer events in our lives.

The prestige of science has misled us into supposing that there is something more metaphysically respectable about atoms than about ambitions; about diagrams than about moods. But the common man knows better and the scientists are beginning to. Space and time, matter and motion, physical circumstances and economic laws — these are the formulas, not the stuff, of our experience. Many a man feels he has moved from shadow to substance at a flash of poetry or at the birth of love. Neither science nor satire can exhaust 'reality' without taking into account those heightened moments in which reality is intimately touched by living men. In those emotions we have come to despise, when our routine moments are ennobled with 'something far more deeply interfused,' an adequate realism will have to find part of its material. For it is among these emotionally heightened moments that all, save a few mocking spirits, find their most adequate life.

HOW TO BE SWEET THOUGH
SOPHISTICATED

ONE can learn as much about the prevailing
temper of a generation by studying its con-
tempts as by remembering its loves. It is indeed very difficult in our time to tell what we
love, the old objects of our adoration having
been riddled with suspicion, and love itself, in
the skeptical hands of our contemporary wise
men, having come into disrepute. To the
Spartan, the ideal of life was represented by
the warrior, disciplined and taut. To the medieval, the ideal of the good life was typified
by the martyr, the ascetic or the saint. In the
Renaissance one wished to be something like
Castiglione's courtier, a polished fusion of the
gentleman, the scholar, the soldier and the
man of the world. The contemporary hero,
the mythical pattern in the imitation of whom
we would live, remains as yet undefined. We
have no hero; what is more to the point, we
suspect hero worship.

But it is only necessary to read the books of
our more circumspect novelists or to move for

an evening in the society of our more intelligent friends, to detect what we do not wish to be, or at least what we do not wish to be thought to be. To the modern spirit, disillusioned or at least unillusioned, the great evil to be avoided is sentimentality. We will forgive almost all sins save those of slushiness. We will condone all defects save those of the soft mind. There is going to be no nonsense about us, and though we may wince a little in private, or cause others to wince in public, we are not going to be children. We are not going to cry for the moon, swear by the stars, or go roller-skating on the rainbow. Not for us the sorrows of Werther, the melancholy of Byron, the purified ecstasies of Coventry Patmore's version, so angelic and so silly, of love. We have both learned and unlearned too much, we think, for that sort of thing. First as to what we have learned.

Science has ceased to be the esoteric possession of experts in a laboratory; it has become the popular jargon of the men in the street or at least of the women in the salon. We know enough about glands to be incredulous of our own or of anybody else's melancholy. When we are depressed we know that it is probably not the cosmos in general but the thyroid in particular that is wrong with us. We are more and more conversant with the chemistry of that clod of clay on a speck of star-dust, that we call human life. We are, therefore, increasingly impatient with the romantic expectation that the universe should conform exactly with the human heart's desire.

Love, again, may among adolescents parade its ancient recognizable rhetoric. But we know better. We see through the disguise, ornate and thin, by which lust conceals itself — even from itself. Every schoolboy, almost, has read Freud. Every adult can quote Havelock Ellis. Our devotion may seem deep, but its depths are in the seamier profundities of our psyches. And as for that eternity with which we credit every passing affection—well, we smile ourselves at that outmoded sentimentalism. Eternal love! Eternal nonsense! A generation that has busied itself with the meaning of time and the flux of consciousness knows enough to discount the permanence of its passions. Another year, another place, and this so vivid absorption will be a memory regarded at best with ironic regret.

Besides all of which, we have lived through a

war and its aftermath. We have learned the hollowness of high-sounding words masking low deeds. We have observed the terrible consequences of acting in a world of brutal fact with soft evasions, with the respectable rubbish of a sentimental moral tradition. We have acquired a wisdom cool and aseptic; we have unlearned the moralities, outwardly benign, actually perilous, on which we were brought up.

So having discarded the old myths, we have gradually been forming a hero-myth of our own. He — or she — we thank the stars (or we would, if we were in a mood to thank anything) is no hero. Every one has met an example of the blue-print Modern acceptable to the contemporary intelligence. It is to be met with at any current social gathering. Enter the Modern. It makes no difference whether it be a man or a woman. In either case, the ideas, like the figure and headdress, will be much the same. He will not talk of love or admit it. He will not believe in the Good Life or be publicly seen leading it. He will have no nonsense about religion or believe that relic of primitive mentality still exists. He will be 'anæsthetized to all that Jesus or that Plato prized.' He will have little patience with politeness or allow himself to practice it. He will try to be a tough mind gayly indifferent in a tough world. The last obscenity he will permit himself will be nobility. The last weakness he will indulge in will be to be sweet or soft. He will talk like a character out of Ernest Hemingway, act like one of Aldous Huxley's bizarre London intelligentsia — or pretend he does — and try to think in such terms as James Joyce's heroines use in their more untrammeled moments.

Now obviously if human nature changes — and it has changed only very little since paleolithic days — it certainly has not gone a complete metamorphosis in the last quarter of a century. Sophisticated people, whatever they may say, have feelings like their more naïve brothers. They love and hate, are stirred to wonder and beauty, hunger and thirst much like the Victorians whom they mock and the living boobies whom they despise. But the new lingo has become a cult and, thanks to the surgical psychologies, the new self-consciousness has become a fashion. It is now in the best circles indecent to be decent, shameful to be shy, offensive to be courteous, suspicious to be simple. Many of our newly smart would rather be found murdering their children than being kind to their parents. They would prefer to be damned for rudeness than to be snickered at for courtesy. They suspect even themselves for any outworn noble sentiment they may happen to experience, any unpremeditated act of kindness they may do, any spontaneous impulse of affection to which they may give way. How many gentle souls does one know who go about being gentle *sub rosa*! How many little amenities of life are people, for fear of being thought ridiculous, beginning to practice behind closed doors. As for love, what roundabout ways a lover will take to express it, for fear that his beloved may set him down as old-fashioned and suburban.

It is not merely fear of what people will say, but fear of what one will think of one's self that makes it difficult in our time to be at once a 'tough mind' and a gentle heart. All the new realism of thinking and writing and conversation have made us self-skeptical. Any one acquainted with the new psychiatry knows why. That gesture we intended to be generous we know to be timid or vain. The kindness we tried to utter we are told is a defense against our own weakness, a fear of not being kind. Enthusiasm is a symptom of prolonged adolescence. Rapture is a psychological debauch that is a vulgar truancy from reason.

Now it would seem to be high time to find out whether this sort of thing has not gone too far. The sophisticates themselves, I suspect, feel that it has. How else is one to account for the joy with which in our most advanced circles, intelligentlemen, intelligentlewomen hail any naïveté in literature or art. Exhibitions of primitive negro sculpture are visited by the best minds. For a season cultivated New York crowded to see a simple little Spanish play entitled 'Cradle Song,' which was compacted of old-fashioned tenderness and peace, a story of simple nuns, their demure ward, and her love-affair, all lavender and lace.

As for the respectable bourgeois rabble whom our sophisticated despise, these comfortable bumpkins cannot get enough of the traditional simple virtues and simple souls. Write them a story, as an Englishman did recently, of a brave father come down in the world, fighting the good fight against slimy obstacles for the love of his pure and devoted son, and you will have hundreds of thousands at your feet and at your publisher's. And what of the whole English-speaking world that quotes with glee the childlike whimsicalities of 'Christopher Robin' and 'Winnie-the-Pooh.'

The question indeed comes down to this: Is it possible to be at once sweet and sophisticated? In our generation can one be at once honest and kindly, intelligent and courteous, informed and gay? Is the price of modern knowledge ill humor and ill temper? Must we pay for having eaten of the tree of good and evil by losing our heritage of urbanity and our saving faith in people and things? Is this the folly that one calls being wise?

These are rhetorical questions and they are intended to be such. This observer at least wishes to bear humble testimony to the conviction that contemporary wisdom has overreached itself. It is submitted that it is the easiest thing in the world, even the contemporary world, to find life agreeable, and to live it agreeably. It is easy to do these things without being a sentimentalist, or what is perhaps the equivalent, without being a fool. I submit that we are the only half-willing followers of fashion when we identify sophistication with the discourteous in manners, the brutal in action and the cynical in thought. It is diffidently proposed that insight into truth, and charm of life need not necessarily be contradictions in terms.

First as to thought! There is a presumption, at once common and fallacious, that to be cynical is by definition to be honest and profound. The young man who has first had his eyes opened to the shallowness and mockery of conventional morals has a fine brusque sense of wisdom at no longer being taken in. He hears the preacher intone, 'Our Father which art in Heaven,' and he thinks of all the human peccadilloes of all the preachers he has ever known. He hears the political orator bellow of justice and the people's rights and his alert memory ruminates upon all the patent injustices of our social order, the travesties of criminal procedure, the mockeries of representative government, the robberies and swinish deceits practiced upon a gullible public. His professors use high words about the Good and he knows and sees what happens daily in the market-place. He hears of the goodness of God and he hears also of wars and rumors of wars and acts of God, floods and earthquakes, that cannot remotely be construed as beneficent.

The honest mind insists, in our generation,

to an unprecedented degree, on being realistic. To be realistic is tantamount to acknowledging that there is a deal of tinsel in our lives and our pretensions. God may still be in His Heaven, but there is more than sufficient evidence that all is not right with the world. But to be realistic is also to admit that an indictment of evils is not the whole story nor the whole universe.

Sophistication demands honesty; it does not require ill temper. There is a kind of wisdom called mellowness and the history of literature is amiably strewn with its exemplars. Montaigne is the prince of these; his essays are the perfectly urbane expression of a man who kept his mind clear and his blood sweet. He knew as well as the latest contemporary futilitarian knows how much there is to bewail in the world. At its best life is short; half of its felicities are illusions and the other half are fatal in their consequences. There is little of which we can be certain, and much of which we must be regretful or ashamed.

But it is not clear now as it was to Montaigne that ill temper is hardly the mood with which to live pleasantly, nor the spirit which reason will commend to adopt toward the world. The light may have gone out of Heaven and meaning out of the earth. We may be fated animals crawling anxiously through the palpitation brief and confused, that we call life. But that chaotic interval is at moments clear with wonder or beauty, and even the disorder of our current societies permits moments of delight. These are clearly on the debit side of the ledger, and a realism that denies the doughnut in affirming the hole is both jaundiced and dishonest.

Nor is it any more honest or reasonable to be continually suspicious of our pleasures, our kindnesses or our raptures because the laboratory has been revealing the machinery by which these operate. Love, we are told, is merely a matter of glandular secretions. But to admit the truth of this physiological fact is far from denying that love exists. There may be a thousand subconscious reasons why we aid a friend in distress or sacrifice our life and energies for some lost or forlorn ideal. The causes of the late war may be demonstrated to have been sordid and mean, but even the most cynical will not deny that thousands of men gave their lives in the generous belief that they were not. It matters not what produces our raptures or our loves or loyalties. Even the most hardened can hardly contest their existence.

To know the material origins of our flights is not to deny their being or their value. To recognize the horrors and evils in the texture of existence is not to blind us to all the loveliness and liveliness there is to enjoy and to commemorate under the sun. It may be said indeed that the essence of being adult rather than childish is to cease to be sulky and irritable at finding life and existence to be what they are. It means among other things to be able to face life steadily and without illusion — but also without disillusion.

And once one has surrendered the cult of disillusion it will not seem necessary any longer to parade a hard-boiled manner, a tough language, and a sour mind. Many of our contemporaries are disappointed sentimentalists who try to conceal from their public their disappointment by the language of the prize-ring or the gutter. Those who have really learned to look candidly upon existence will not need to apologize for their candor with fighting words. If life is really tragic, we are all in the same boat, and the least we can do is to greet each other *pro tem* with a decent courtesy, if only to mitigate by friendliness the dark interval in which we live. It will not seem necessary to those truly gifted with a tragic sense of life to use the language of the street to prove they are not sentimental. No one was more profoundly candid about the universe than Thomas Hardy. No one had a gentler tongue. Nor is it necessary, finally, to be rough-neck in one's thinking. There is after all, little use in defying a universe that is *a priori* defined as indifferent.

Sentimentalism is usually attibuted to a prolonged adolescence, a perpetual refusal to emerge from the mirage of cherished illusions to the candid prospect of realities. But the convention has risen in our own day that cynicism or perpetual disillusion is the symptom of maturity. The fallacy of sentimentalism is that it paints to itself a picture that conforms comfortably with its own roseate desires. The fallacy of cynicism is that it paints the universe as in league against human ideals. A persistent satire upon life is hardly more adult than a persistent prettifying of it. One of the worst sins Dante could think of was to sulk in the sunlight. To those who did he assigned the eternal punishment of wallowing in the mud. To be understanding is to be equable, and to be equable is to escape the need for being smart or sulky or hard. 'Heartbreak,' says a character in Shaw's 'Heartbreak House,' 'is the end of happiness and the beginning of peace.' If our hearts were at peace, we should not need to put up so elaborate a smoke-screen of pert defense. We should not need to insist on singing our satirical praises to a God from whom all evils flow. We should not need to think of existence as a psychiatric clinic, nor to be its perpetual *enfants terribles*.

One might set up as a conceivable ideal for our generation the combination of the tough mind and the gentle heart. The tough mind will be undismayed by any fact or any horror; it will not be misled by any pleasure or mirage. It will know that man is neither an ape nor an angel, but a precarious and harassed animal living in an uncertain, sometimes abominable, sometimes exquisite world. The gentle heart will know how far even lust and hypocrisy have their understandable causes. It will know enough to discern good and forgive evil. Some one once called John Stuart Mill 'the saint of rationalism.' The ideal of character for our generation, for any generation, is, perhaps, a union of the reasoner and the saint. Reason has led men into inhumanity; religion has led them into illusion. A fusion of the two spirits may be possible in an age that has learned to think candidly and has, since we are still human, not forgotten how to feel.

One has an image of what that modern type of the 'high-minded man' will be like. He is to be met with at least in potentiality in some of the educated youth of our own day. I have known a dozen myself, young men and women who were not fooled by ancient illusions, were not hardened by a modern cult. Their minds were steel-like in their precision and taut in their honesty. Their hearts were, like those that Dante valued, gentle. They could relish the goods of life without blinding themselves to its nightmares. They could discern the tragedy of existence and laugh at its diversions. Of such, as it was said of old, may be the Kingdom of Heaven. From such may be forming the modern temper.

SPECULATIONS

RELIGION AND THE PHILOSOPHICAL IMAGINATION

THE relations between philosophy and religion have always been extremely confused and obscure. Religion appears to be connected on the one hand with the deeply irrational needs and excitements of human nature, and on the other with an assumed supernatural order which brings a deep irrational peace, a quietistic escape from the confusions and frustrations of the natural world. Philosophy has been traditionally concerned with the cool attempt of reason to frame a steady vision of all things in their order and worth. Religion has its roots and sources in a hasty assumption of magical and personally conceived efficacies and in impatient terrors and superstitions. Philosophy is allegedly the product of a deliberate and logical detachment clearly envisaging the ultimate nature of existence.

The relations of religion and philosophy in the past have as a consequence been highly controversial. Philosophy has arisen as a critic of the tangled skeins of myth and magic, of creed and tradition, of private ecstasy and traditional creeds. It has tried to expurgate theology of self-deceptions and logical confusions, or to explain away God. Philosophers have been the intellectualistic critics or the intellectualistic apologists for religion. Religions grown self-conscious have turned philosophical and turned mysteries into metaphysics, mystical insights into logistical proofs, the vision of God into a formula of his being. Philosophies have, in the midst of defending or disposing of traditional theological conceptions (or even in ignoring them), found themselves ultimately, in so far as they were more than verbal formulas, precisely such visions of destiny ultimate and moving as constituted the themes of religions.

The long-standing quarrel or the illicit alliances of reason and religion have been due to a singularly literal misapprehension of what the functions of reason and religion are. It has traditionally been assumed that philosophy is a logical demonstration of truth and that religion is a magical revelation of it. From the point of view of a humane observer, committed neither to the exaltation of reason nor to the rationalistic defense of religion, the functions of both must be differently conceived. That technique called reason by which philosophy traditionally has been presumed to demonstrate the truth about the cosmos turns out upon examination of human history and the human scene, turns out, in other words, upon empirical examination, to arise as a practical servile instrument of a perplexed animal in a complex and changing environment. It is that process by which the troubled human creature establishes some operative bases of stability to guide and to prosper it in an uncertain temporal history. That efficacious structure we call 'the world' is a system whose constitution is determined by its relevancy to human needs, by its felicitous practicality. It remains in essence a poetic synthesis, a construct which happens to be useful and auspicious. That it is a poetry, that it is a synthesis, the history of science and philosophy both show. Successive critiques of science have been long laboring in showing the limitations, the relativity, the logical contradictions and defects of that world of space and time on which the dogmatic mechanist has so long been content to estimate all rival forms of truth. Science has given us a figment now become so routine that we lapse

into calling it reality. Kant elaborately eluci-
dated the simple position that it is a figment
whose structure is determined by the subject
for which it appears. The world of appearances
is no less an apparition because it is so dependable, so steady, and so clear. But it is not necessarily an apparition in the sense that it may
be conceived of as being the provincial poetic
surrogate for the Unknowable, a Reality which
in the common and determined garb of the
known world of science became an object of
knowledge. It is an apparition, rather as a
work of art is an apparition. It is the product
of a creative intelligence, a dream whose categories are determined by practical reference
and mundane utility.

The imagination has been discounted by
philosophers and scientists because they have
felt a moral necessity for identifying the co-
herent dream of mechanism or the self-consist-
ent fiction of a metaphysical construction with
an ultimate reality and an unimpeachable
truth. The naturalistic mechanist and the
absolute idealist have confused the activity of
creative cosmic fiction with the process of veri-
fiable discovery. What is really the work of
synthesizing imagination they have held to be

the activity of a discriminating analytical inquiry.

It is on the basis of the hypostasis which philosophers and scientists have made of their particular fictions of reality that they have defended or condemned religion. Religion and science, religion and philosophy have been two fables that have quarreled with each other to be called unmistakable descriptions of authentic being. And on the basis of practicality the dream of science has certainly had the advantage. In comparison with its sober mechanical categories, the flaming mythologies, the dramatic histories, the melodramatic systems of salvation of religion have seemed false, irrelevant, misleading and insecure. They were at best promises of a world that was not here, images of a world that was not now. Their histories could be shown to be lies, and their prophecies were always half suspected to be so. At least science could always be checked up by the senses and by its diurnal efficacy; metaphysics could offer clear and distinct ideas and at least demonstrate a world that could not be discovered. Religion had ultimately always to refer to some special and suspect avenue of revelation, or to a special organ of insight that must to reason and the senses remain more than half suspect.

The whole study of religion is illuminated when it is seen that those versions of life and nature that go by the name of religion, like those versions of nature that go by the name of science or metaphysics, are complex poetic fictions, which in the case of religions become socialized, systematized, become a doctrine, a ritual, and a church. The imaginative character of scientific and philosophical systems is forgotten because their language and their temper is that of prose. Both are themselves suspicious of those flights into worlds not here and memories and promises of wonders not now, of those humane and dramatic categories in which religious eloquence has been traditionally prone to read nature. The imaginative character of religious systems, histories, dogmas, and rituals is forgotten, because each religion comes to its adherents and its destroyers with the soothing or provoking certificate of a divine revelation. It is the voice of revealed truth, not the poetry of human aspiration, of longings for other worlds and the desire through some seduction of sense or imagination to escape from this. Both the rationalistic philosopher and the reasoning theologian have taken themselves and each other literally. In taking their own word for what they were doing, they have failed to recognize what was being done.

The business of an emancipated philosopher, emancipated that is, from literalness in both religion and philosophy, would appear to be something different from arguing a case for or against what religion says, and seeing rather what it is or does. It would appear to be his concern to follow each religious tradition, its doctrine, its ritual and its organization, to the human courses and motives out of which these have grown, to the ideals of which they are the embodiment, and to the social consequences that each imaginative version of life and nature has for its believers. Philosophy must cease to treat as formulas what is really a high and consequential form of art. It must cease to criticize on the grounds of truth and falsity what is rather estimable and appreciable as a metaphor. It is a metaphor, too, that lingers largely because it so aptly reveals some native tendency, some characteristic tragedy, some permanent hope or despair of the human spirit. We live in a world where all discourse is metaphor and where the metaphors of religion have been curiously congenial and luminous articulations of what science is not interested in uttering and what metaphysics is too abstract and general to express.

The history of religion, thus sympathetically and liberally surveyed, is the history of variegated embodiments of human ideals of a perfect world, of perfect beings, and of perfect peace. In a sense it is the history of the ways of life, not of ways of life here and now, but for and in eternity. It is the history of the imagination in a more passionate and poetical form than is the history of speculation. What in philosophy is an intimation of the absolute, in religion is a vision of God, what in Greek speculation is *physis* or the movement of nature, in Greek mythology is the chariot of Apollo crossing the Heavens and thus lighting the earth, or Poseidon agilely stirring or benignantly calming the sea; what in medieval speculation is the absolute intellectual identification with God, in Dante's 'Paradiso' is the vision of the Mystic Rose. What in Greek philosophy is a sober discourse on a prudent way of life in this world in the Greek mysteries is an ecstatic invitation to a transcendent way of life in another.

The imagination in both philosophy and religion has its law; in philosophy they are those of an inner consistency or a pragmatic reference; of logical order or of practical verifiability. The imagination in religion has its laws likewise, but they are those determined neither by the canons of logic or of practical efficacy. They are constituted by the needs and fears, the hopes and the frustrations of that spirit which the body and necessity permit, for a brief time to flower. The consistency of the world of the religious imagination is congruity with the native impulses of the human spirit and some compensation for its natural defeats. That is why for all the variegated language of religion, its themes remain substantially the same; its logic almost identical. If philosophy is a way of life and science a way of control, religion is a way of escape and a way of salvation. It is escape from the uncertainty, the transiency, the moral meaninglessness of a world to one whose geography is composed of desiderated perfections and whose meaning is secured by the presence of a God, a purpose, and a pattern.

Once religion is conceived of as a lyrical and dramatic symbolism by which the significance of life, the movement of nature, the aim and direction of human action are represented, the whole approach to theology, to ritual, and to ecclesiastical organization is transformed. Theology, whatever its alleged and official function, turns out to be in essence and in actuality, the formulas by which life tries to express its notion of a perfect being, of the relation of man to that perfection, and the methods by which man may be redeemed from fact to the experience of pure ideality. Ritual ceases to be what Euthyphro defined it to be in Plato's dialogue, 'a commerce with divinity.' It is not a practical technique by which the gods may be coerced. It is a symbolic ceremonial by which the individual crises of experience, birth, the beginnings of adolescence, marriage, death, the renascence of nature in spring, and the death of things in autumn are raised from their momentary and meaningless provincialism to the significance and status of the eternal. The physical fact of birth is for example in the Christian tradition made by baptism into a sacrament. It is an imaginative ceremonial rendering of the dual fact that man as a creature is born to the chaos and corruption of life, but that through interceding grace he may be redeemed to that pure and immortal essence which is his ideal possibility. The Eucharist makes eating of bread and drinking of wine a kindly self-deception by which the life and death of one man in history is made the pattern, the example, and the instrument of redemption of all men through eternity.

There is a picture in the Vatican Gallery at Rome that admirably illustrates the significance of those poetic forms of idealized life which religions have called paradise. It is the 'Trinita' by Raphael. In the lower half of the picture are a group of theologians discussing theology; in the upper panel is a vision of God surrounded by saints and angels. That vision above is the object of adoration; it is the theme of all the discourse below. Just as ritual is a symbolic representation of the significance of crucial episodes in experience, so theology breaks occasionally beyond the bonds of that logic which constitutes its technique to that imagery and music which construct a world of supernatural reality out of the happiest materials, the brightest scintillations of that actual world which philosophers and theologians like to call appearance. The Greek gods, all celerity in movement, swiftness, clarity, and light, are human beings as they would wish themselves to be and as they therefore imagine the Greek gods to be forever; the Olympian family is what might be described as Greek sculpture turned into theological eternities (much indeed as Platonic ideas may be described as Greek marble turned into eternal essences). The forms of art become quintessentialized into the Forms of Aristotle, the serene and winning forms of life become the gods of the Pantheon.

In the more tragic epic we call Christianity there is an idealization not simply of the felicities of life, but a poignant rendering of its tragedy in the eternal and invariant terms of pity and redemption. It is no longer a question to the interested observer of the human scene whether Christ lived or not or whether through the intercession of Christ man may not be saved. The whole touching story of a god become man that man may be saved is paraphrased in the symbols, mythical and humane, of what the limitations of life are and what its fulfillments may be. It is a way of saying what intelligence finds to be true, that the human creature the victim at once of his own blindness and of the order of Nature, futile and uncaring, out of nature and his own will cannot be saved. There is no moral reason why massive blind corruption should be saved, nor any mechanical certainty that nature will trouble about his salvation. If salvation is to come at all, it can only come as an act of grace, and on the ground of pity. If it is to be achieved, it can only be so by a force transcending the careless chaos or the merely random order of nature. All this is what the myth of Christ symbolically states. Christ saved man not because he deserved it, but out of pity. Man could not be saved by nature alone, but only by God. Take the myth as true and it becomes a highly controversial hypothesis; take it as false and the meaning of the myth is obscured and forgotten. Take it for what it is, a picture rather than a proof, a moral persuasion rather than an argument, and it becomes part of those variegated constructions by which the mind of man has tried to render the flux and tragedy, the fulfillments and stabilities of life intelligible to his own spirit.

So far in this paper, religion has been treated as a form of the imagination and the imagination has been treated as a soliloquy, and it undoubtedly remains true that out of whatever common and communal conditions and crises of experience religious myths, rituals, and theologies arise, their characteristic formulas must always have occurred to those rare beings one calls prophetic geniuses. If religion is a form of poetry, the authors of its classic expression must certainly have been poets. It remains true likewise that however complex the intellectual doctrine, however complicated the ecclesiastical machinery by which this poetry becomes socialized into a cult, a church, or a tradition, its net effect upon a believer is the effect of a soliloquy personally relived — the drama of Christ's life becomes the drama of the inner conflict of the individual soul. The society of happy saints who constitute paradise is for the aspiring believer a society in which his own citizenship happily prefigures. That is why William James was justified in his extremely individualistic treatment of religion. Where it is genuine, religion is a personal search for a personal salvation. The history of religion might from one aspect be adequately treated as the history of religious poets and those readers and believers whom they have moved.

None the less it is impossible to treat reli-

gion from this separatistic soliloquizing angle
alone. What distinguishes religion from mere
poetry is not simply that its themes are more
grandiose and comprehensive than that of
most poets. It is poetry not simply as a private
experience casually disseminated, but a common tradition publicly and deliberately propa-
gated and maintained. The burden of human
experience finds prophetic genius to express it
in a myth, a message or a doctrine. The crises
of human life generate a characteristic ritual
by which these crises are met, universalized and
expressed. But the prophecy becomes a doctrine, the message becomes a catechism, the
myth becomes sacred history. These are a social property, a social possession, a patrimony.
They demand organization, exposition, official
communication; they generate a priesthood
and an official religious society, the church.
Nothing would on its surface seem to be far-
ther removed from poetry or prophecy than a
cult or a church. Yet these are simply evidence of how seriously the poetry, the prophecy, and the message of religions have been
taken by human beings. Religion is not simply
imagination, but imagination social in its origins and its consequences. The church is the

organ of a cosmic poetry become controlling and traditional in the lives of millions of believers. Just in the same way therefore as it would display a singularly illiberal lack of understanding to condemn religious doctrine for literal falsity, so it would display an equal lack of sympathetic temper to condemn or criticize ecclesiastical institutions on the basis of their purely material embodiment or consequences. The church is simply the stumbling human attempt to take its religious idealizations seriously and to take them seriously by giving them a form, a public status, to make them communicable. The error of religion and of critics of religion has been to estimate ideal constructions by criteria of facts. In other words to take metaphors as dogmas. The error of criticism of ecclesiastical institutions (and of their defenders) has been to take them as privileged bureaucracies instead of as organs through which private visions or moving social traditions might be made permanent, contagious, and secure. When Saint Augustine long ago made the church on earth the earthly incarnation or manifestation of the City of God, he was giving it perhaps a place that it in fact does not deserve. But Saint Augustine was a

Platonist and one must take his statement platonically. He was in essence simply calling attention to the fact that the church is, in any religion, that society by which God, heaven and salvation cease to be personal vagaries or hysterias and become the common property of mutually sympathetic human intelligences. The anomalous position of the church lies in the fact that, though its mind and its imagination are in heaven, its property is on earth and its officials are all of necessity earthly. It becomes tangled up in the politics and temporal confusions, the dishonesties, the prejudices, and the passions of that world in the midst of which it is supposed to stand as the emblem, the banner, the organ, and the social expression of the city of God. In its hands a poetical mystery tends to become an exclusive secret possession; its ritual ceases to be a symbolism and turns into a legalism precise, rigid and cruel, as it did in the hands of the Pharisees. It becomes simply one more form of earthly bureaucracy instead of a society of common worship and a common hunger for salvation.

All this does, I think, serve to explain why the approach from the institutional side of religion has always so repelled the sensitive and made the rational impatient. The sensitive to whom religion is an experience of life in its more heroic and ideal aspects have been rebuffed by the official literal-mindedness of an organized hierarchy placed between them and their vision of God. The rationalists have seen in religious institutions the vested interests of a propertied or official class, have dismissed the hierarchy of cults and churches as a lover of learning might dismiss the administration of a university. They have forgotten that the human being even in his religious moments is not a soliloquizing poet, but is always a half-lonely member of a group whose contagion and moral support he desires. Even the hermit in his imagination lives in the society of saints in heaven. Even the monk has his companions, and the philosopher his friends and correspondents. The poetry of religion, concerned as it is with so many issues involving other people, demands the presence of other people, through amiable and actual connivance for the expression of that emotion which the symbols of religion arouse. It is a need of social sanction and support and communal expression that has always tended to make mysticism, the most private of experiences, turn so rapidly into a mystery cult. It is what has kept Protestantism, so individualistic in its theory, so persistently social in its practice. It has been the basis of the fact that Christianity has never been simply the Christian soliloquy, but has been the constantly reënacted drama of the Mass by the Church.

To the philosopher, therefore, the history of religion demands attention as a symbolism of three levels of expression. First, what one might call the pure poetry of religion, the actual content and imaginative significance of those images of heaven, those ways of redemption, those avenues of escape which are doctrines and pictures in the religious patrimony. These must be treated as typical poetical embodiments of the way in which the private imagination has reacted to the ideal hopes and the tragic frustrations of life in the world. In religion all these items, literally taken, go by the name of theology. Secondly, the philosopher is concerned with the symbolism present in ritual and in ceremony, the expression in act of that poetry which in contemplation constitutes the objects of religious theory and vision. Thirdly, the philosopher must see the church, any church, in terms of that traditional patrimony of which it is the social communicant of expression, and recognize the imaginative necessity and consequences of that public association which it has. Seen in this light much of the quarrel between religion and science, much of the antipathy between philosophy and religion become otiose and irrelevant.

Seen in this light also, much of the criticism of ecclesiastical institutions and much of their defense lose their point. The institutions through which the creative and traditionalized imagination become operative are like all institutions subjected to the vicissitudes and corruptions of their members and their mechanisms. It was Voltaire who said that if there had been no God, it would have been necessary to invent one. It might be added that if the religious imagination had no church, it would be necessary to find one. The poetry of religious vision is a culture trait of that social background and cultural history which finds in revelations and apocalypses, in mystical visions, and in consistent logical doctrine its imaginative embodiment. This embodiment would remain private, transient, and obscure if it were not clarified and given repeated communal expression, and the way of communal expression is in the service and ritual of a creed and a church. There is a bleak and lonely beauty in the picture of the saint communicating directly with his God, but the content of his vision, and the structure of his paradise will be derived very largely from the corner of earth, the inhabitants, and the social tradition from which his poetry must perforce borrow its symbols. That vision itself would be forgotten or unintelligible save that it brought to focus the common aspirations of many minds moved by an identically intelligible symbolism, built upon commonly understandable and appreciable hopes and fears, triumphs and defeats. Religion turns out upon examination, then, to be something more than a personal hysteria or excitement, something more than a private and incommunicable literature of escape. It is rather the language by which any social group through some of its inspired representatives frames a vision of an ideal society, a paradisial citizenship, in which all the members of a given group can in imaginative anticipation live. One might indeed reverse Saint Augustine: the church is not the earthly embassy of the City of God, the City of God is the ideal object which becomes vivid and communicable through creeds and rituals, the dogmas, the formulas, the forms of worship in which a social group manages to articulate its vision.

Religion thus conceived is the poetry of the race objectified into dogma and transmitted through a church revivified now and then through the appearance of those geniuses of fresh insight who go by the name of prophets or heretics. The limitations of religion, its cruel blindnesses and bigotries, the false hopes it has led men to entertain, the narrowness it has persuaded them to practice, all find explanation. The failures of religion are the failures of a social imagination that cannot help reflecting the crudenesses and provincialisms of the level or quality of culture that gives it birth. The beauty of religion and, in a profound sense, its permanent truth lie in the fact that whatever defects the expression of religion in any period or in any church has, its intentions have always been cosmic, moral and fundamental. It has been the stammering human periphrasis for a private and instant vision of what existence purified and cleared of its dross might be. Christianity, Buddhism, the religions of Persia and Egypt, the inflexible monotheism of the

Jews, the militant monotheism of the Moham-
medans have all been special and local dialects
of a common language. They have been the
vocabularies in which the heart of man has
tried to comfort itself, ways of escape from the
natural world, visions of a world to which the
distilled spirit might arrive through grace or
sacrifice, through asceticism and abnegation,
through penance or good works or disciplined
contemplation.

It remains to be noted, among many other
things, that the traditional dialects in which
the persistent imagination of religion has
uttered itself, have become difficult, irrelevant,
many minds provoking. They have been taken
so literally that for many people their symbolism is irrecoverable. The Ptolemaic astro-
nomy in its conflict with the Copernican has
obscured the moral significance, the symbolic
suasion of Christian imagery and doctrine.
The clear and intense dichotomies between
good and evil ways of life which constitute the
heart of prophetic Judaism have been hidden
by the now otiose and incredible Mosaic cos-
mogony. But the human need for expressing
the tribulations and the ideals of human experience still persists. The light may be out of

241

the old heavens and a darkness over a natural-istically conceived earth. But the classic pre-dicaments and aspirations that generated the old mythologies and doctrines still endure. Neither death nor defeat, neither life nor de-sire, have faded from the natural scene.

It goes not quite without saying that our new knowledge and unprecedented cultural situation, the technologies that form the con-ditions, the moral confusions that are their bitter and confusing fruit, will need to frame somewhat differently, will necessarily differ-ently express the salvation we are seeking, the corruption and destruction which we are seek-ing to avoid. The newer metaphysics too has determined a different angle of vision, and will have to find a differently uttered object of as-piration. For the old world of fixity and de-termination, we have begun to substitute not a reality, but a process, a continuous and crea-tive experience, all growth and freedom, in which intelligence has a possible and a positive rôle, the rôle of constantly varying experience itself, so that a remote and paradisial possibil-ity of to-day becomes the enrichment of to-morrow. The new technology, the consequent social disintegrations, and moral chaos of a

society physically efficient and spiritually dis-
organized develop their own special problems,
their own unprecedented hopes. The new wisdom which sees Time not as devouring its
children, but generating ever fairer possible
progeny will have to find emotional expression
in new forms. The new world and its dispensa-
tions have produced hitherto impossible visions
of more possible worlds. The old images of
Heaven and salvation will not do where Heaven
is no longer found in peace, but in adventure;
salvation not in the rapt and static contemplation of the eternal, but in the creative arts of
life. At some not remote date, when the whole
impact of the newer movements in thought,
the as yet spiritually unassimilated conditions
of life may have become part of the daily imagination, as they have already become part of
the daily routine of contemporary society, a
new set of symbols will arise, words that are
not meaningless transferences from a setting
that is past and illusions that are gone, but
that arise out of the promptings of current
experience itself. We are at present living, to
paraphrase Matthew Arnold's phrase, between
two religions, one dead and one powerless to be
born. Or to put it more precisely, between one

dying and of irrelevance, and one yet to be
more than an infantile hungering after speech.

In this period it would be impossible and im-
proper for a philosopher, with his eye turned
upon eternity, to speculate about a future or a
past which under the eye of eternity is non-
existent. But the philosopher can look at the
future not with eyes of a prophetic determinist,
but with the eyes of a dramatic poet. He can
at least imagine the kind of religion that a
future arising out of the present situation
would need, and at least look back with retrospective sympathy at a religion whose date but
not whose wisdom is altogether in the past.
For free as contemporary thinking may be of
traditional illusions or vanished forms of life
and society, practice and art, the old symbols
are not altogether meaningless to us. Nor is it
likely that whatever the religion of the future
may be (and that there will be none is to as-
sume the end of all art and imagination and
science and thought as well) or whatever the
inanition of present religion is, the old symbols
are without their depths, their induplicable
wisdom, their as yet unparalleled insight and
tenderness about the ultimate hopes of mankind. In their myth and magic once literally

244

taken, he will find a patrimony of images. He will find in them expressions of those classic predicaments which human creatures in any age and under any formulas of thought find themselves in. No optimistic radiance about the control of nature or the discipline of human nature can altogether cloud that tragedy of necessity or confusion, that thirst for freedom and clarity, which have informed so much of traditional mythology. Classic forms of art have survived unprecedented changes in existence. Greek marbles and Christian painting have not become unappreciable or unintelligible in a world given over to industry and empire. There is no reason to believe that classic forms of religion, the most serious forms of human art involving the widest passions and issues, have become unintelligible to an age which has new problems and a new vocabulary. The modernist critic need not be misled into dismissing these ancient enshrinements of inexpugnable human crises as true or in condemning them as idolatries. These embodiments of the hopes and difficulties of dead societies are neither simply beautiful nor simply dead. They are part of the continuing imagination, the living social heritage. They may function as living words and images, more living because of their mellowed associations, along with new words and unantedated images. Out of all this may be constructed a religion, a relevant body of metaphor to express contemporary knowledge, contemporary needs, and contemporary loyalties and devotions. These in their deeper rangings will be found to be not dissimilar from those of human beings with other problems and other languages and other symbols, but with crises we can recognize and urgencies like our own.

What this poetic embodiment of our own age will be it would require at once a prophet and poet to suggest. Just as the mediæval theologian suggested God by negatives, so perhaps this possible religion will be suggestible here. It will be without traditional unctions or falsities. It will not try to cloud inquiry by the noxious clinging to false illusions by faith. Its church will have to be free of all hierarchy, exclusiveness or possessiveness. This church will have to have a ritual that will not be an artifice of illicit science, a magical device. Its positive content, its auspicious ritual, its organization are for that not impossible religious genius who in the very midst of our confusions may arise to find the liberating words that will meet our new situations and the ancient hungers of our being. Whatever it is, it will function as religion has always functioned, as the poetic translation of experience, as that by which, in the old language, a man lives, that in imagination, and by which the deeper currents of his practice are controlled. Its ritual will be concerned with those forms of art which comprise the aspirations of life. Its church will be a holy place, holy in no dread and barbarous sense of a tabooed spot, but holy in that it is the society, the communion, like that of the players in a Greek tragedy, which expresses what is most central and moving in the hearts of its communicants. God will perhaps be unimaginably different from anything the tradition-cramped minds of men thus far have found to express. Salvation will be no conventional hypostasis of rest or thought. There will be perhaps a high element of adventure and excitement in the peace it offers. But God, however he be called or defined, salvation, however be it denominated or described, will be what they will provide.

That religion in some such sense will persist is questionable only by those who believe that long before the earth will have frozen forever, the heart of man will have frozen, and with it that happy process of imagination by which that heart has fulfilled those of its longings which nature or current society denied, that happy process by which a meaning is read into experience, and that meaning is found good.

ADAM, THE BABY, AND THE MAN FROM MARS

ADAM, the Baby, and the Man from Mars have always been invoked in the history of thought as the only three unprejudiced observers of the human scene — Adam, fresh from the hand of his Maker, the Baby new to earth and sky, and the Man from Mars on his first visit to an alien planet. Thus have three fantastic psychologies been invoked as the basis of far more than that number of fantastic metaphysics. The adult, civilized, earthbound philosopher has tried to conceive three beings minus his own normal illusions. These three noetic legends have been as good and as far as thought could reach in the way of absolutes.

Adam has been the symbol of an adult intelligence, uncorrupted by previous history or acquired error, waking to a universe whose order is already fixed, and whose opportunities await his enjoyment and his understanding. The Baby is the untrained educable organ of experience, born into an established world it must gradually learn to comprehend. (Of course the Baby has varied considerably in the History of Thought, but its symbolic function has remained largely the same; only the blankness of its mind or its original capacities for learning have theoretically varied.) The Man from Mars has been the nearest to a genuine surrogate for an Absolute. Here is a creature with an intelligence presumably different from that current in sublunar regions and presumably different in its history, and subjected, therefore, to none of our major provincialisms. It has come into a cosmos whose conditions it must presumably find novel, and whose concerns it can obviously regard with detachment. Its own logic need be conceived as modified only sufficiently to enable it to comprehend a world whose intelligibility is in terms of an intelligence organized differently than its own. The Man from Mars must remain Martian, but he must become, within limits and *pro tem*, a Human.

Adam may be said to have been always the symbol of intellectual innocence and noetic integrity; the Baby of plasticity; the Man from Mars of detachment. Of course it goes without saying that writers have constantly read into these creatures all manner of human prejudices and presumptions. Adam, the Baby, and the Man from Mars have, indeed, usually been no other than their very human expositors. The true Absolute, as idealists have wisely insisted, would be the Mind of God, but even into God human prejudices have perforce been read. God thinks the thoughts of Hegel or Royce as the case may be. In any case, Adam, the Baby, and the Man from Mars are more appreciably human, and hence more easily conceivable. No thinker can easily read himself into the innocence of the first, the plasticity of the second, or the detachment of the third. The first two are more frequently imitated than the third. It may be emancipating, however, to see what the world might look like to these three putative observers, and what their philosophies, if they had any, might be. Perhaps if one could combine innocence, plasticity, and detachment, one might begin to be a philosopher. But let us examine the classic example of each in turn.

Adam is, at first blush, the ideal illustration of uncorrupted intelligence. For here is an adult creature with ready-made habits of observation and full-blown capacities for inference. His mind (one had best examine him first in his familiar historic situation) was a *tabula rasa* as far as information or ideas were concerned. He was fresh in the sense that he had not been exposed to the idols of the marketplace. Being grown up, he might be expected to have been stimulated by nature to thought. Made in the image of his Maker, it was natural that he should respond to the stimulation of nature with untroubled directness of observation and uncorroded clarity of inference. He was a philosopher without traditions and a poet without inherited clichés. 'Experience knocked authoritatively at his door.' Yonder rose was there to be seen, not to be doubted, nor to be whisked away into nothingness by an inherited dialectical technique. It was to be smelled, not to be accounted for, or to be explained away. All the objects of perception were free from any memorial taints of past apprehensions, though they were immediately apprehensible. They were free even of names, which, it will be remembered, Adam had to give them for purposes of reference and recognition. Adam is the purest example of pure experience. But it will be well to see from what impurities his experience was free:

In the first place, from that first roseate

awakening to a dew drenched reality, he was doubtless too busy learning to know the world to question whether it were knowable. What impinged upon his senses, provoked his mind to reflection, or accelerated the beating of his heart, could not be for him a doubtful world of shadows or illusion. He was the first naturalist in philosophy because he met nature in its own terms. There was no veil of verbal tradition between himself and the facts. He knew even the conventionality of names; had he not given them himself? But he knew also the stability of nature since the objects to which he gave names turned up with a certain recognizable regularity, each after its kind. The evenings and mornings in the Garden of Eden had their obvious rhythmic succession; the animals their fixed habits; his own body its unvarying cycle of freshness and fatigue and repose and freshness again. How could he question the reality of life — or of love — in the presence of Eve, or those trees whose fruits he ate or desired.

Out of his steadily increasing store of virgin impressions and effective habits, he might have framed eventually a sound, and, in so far as his experience went, a complete philosophy. For it would have been based on an accurate geography of the Garden of Eden, and on its history, contemporaneous with his own. His theory of knowledge would have been relevant, had he troubled to have one. It would have been no theory at all, but simply a report of what he knew, and the specific ways in which he had come to know it. His metaphysics would, I think, have been clear; it would have been merely a statement of the most general conditions of that happy world in which he found himself living.

There would, I think, have been one notable omission in his thought, though one cannot be sure that it ought to be classed as a defect — by any one save a moralizing philosopher. There would have been no ethics in his system. For a perfect world would not generate moralizing philosophers. At most it would generate only poets commenting with vivid precision on the felicities of things. Adam, moved to expression, might have made poetry whose theme would have been his whole cosmic setting, a hymn to all being, which was all good. But his images would not have been tinctured with morals. For, it must be remembered, he was living in a world whose elements were choice and whose organization was flawless. With

him, in the words of the schools, the realm of
existence and the realm of value were identical
— unless, it be held, as indeed Adam seems to
have held, that one prohibition could invalidate
a Paradise. If he had not eaten of the Tree of
Good and Evil, it would never have occurred
to him that evils were there to be remedied or
problems to be solved. A clear intelligence
moving always in an order where there were no
discomforts and no traditions, might never,
nay would never, have dreamed of moral
theory. Even if morals be, as we are told at
present, completely social in their origins,
there could have been no problem of moral
adjustment for Adam and Eve, all of whose
relations with one another flowed not from
necessity, but from love. In no important
human sense could Adam have been an idealist.
Why, where there was continuous bliss, should
one be perplexed about changes, or imagine
necessity for change? Where all is good, there
can be no question as to evil, no query as to its
origin or concern for its abatement.

Though in the Garden of Eden Adam might
never have been provoked to moral theory, he
might very well have been tempted toward an
æsthetics. But this would have been no doctri

naire system crammed on to alluring facts. It would have been at most an attempt to distinguish with precision and with luminous appreciation the varied forms and volumes of pleasure and delight. All his philosophy might, indeed, have been naught but an æsthetics, *theory*, *theoria*, in the fine unspoilt sense of a steady vision of things.

Perhaps it is only in the Garden of Eden, a cosmos composed of goods, that a philosophy of pure sight and clear inference is possible at all. Moving exclusively in a realm consisting of values, Adam would never have been able to make the mistake of confusing facts with ideals. With him the identification would not have been dangerous; it would have been true. With us where values are happy accidents or hard precarious achievements, the identification of the two is fatal. It brings values no nearer, and leaves existence no whit improved. Adam was living in such cosmic circumstances as idealists, by the *force majeure* of an optimistic logic, try to convince us that we also are enjoying. Adam's fusion of facts and ideals would have been merely the innocence of happy accuracy; for us in our less smooth state to imitate him would have all the dangers of sentimental fiction. Philosophical idealists are indulging in a metaphysics that would have been relevant only before the Fall of Man.

There seems reason to suppose that if Adam had lived long enough in the Garden of Eden (and except for Eve he might have), he would have produced a sound enough metaphysics. He could certainly have pushed experience back to its irreducible constituents, the ineluctable elements of existence and the primary forms of his understanding of them. If it be protested that the integrity of his whole philosophy would have been vitiated because it was accepted on a naïve faith in God, it must be remembered that the creation which he accepted on faith was borne witness to no less by his senses and his heart. The Word had already become flesh in the world which he saw about him, and the faith which he was asked to accept was none other than that which the unambiguous conditions of his existence verified. If he had no epistemological difficulties, it was because he had less reason even than Berkeley to believe that God would tantalize him with illusion. He had, moreover, no tradition of words to place between himself and the honest scrutiny of things.

The Adam usually invoked, of course, as the impartial observer of the human scene is not Adam in the Garden of Eden, but Adam in the forests of the secular world. He is simply the noble savage. To be truly Adam out of the Garden of Eden, he would have to be Adam after the Fall. He would have to be conceived as having known Eden, and as contrasting it with his unhappier lot in a blasted world. Adam, after the Fall, is the perplexed *genus humanis*. Any philosophy he developed after that catastrophe would be dictated by necessity and nostalgia. His ideals would be the images of a Paradise regained. They would be those of any harassed mortal dreaming himself into equilibrium. Morals would become an issue for him. He would constantly have to choose the lesser of two evils; he would have to learn some way of sacrificing immediate pleasures for permanent goods; to reconcile his nature with the nature of things, subtly accommodating himself to the one and reluctantly modifying the other. His metaphysics would be clouded by wishful illusions, and his healthy animal faith corrupted by sick verbal doubts. He would seek to account for evil and to talk himself into the omnipresence of good. In a short time he would be the typical tangled modern philosopher.

But the Adam envisaged as the uncorrupted observer is not an Adam with memories and regrets, an exile from an Eden. He is simply an innocent trying to understand and adjust himself to a very different order from that upon which the Adam of tradition opened his eyes. He would be simple, but he would not be born into a simple world. He would be without malice, but the conditions of his existence would not be innocuous. He would merely bring to bear the simplicity of an Adam before the Fall upon a situation that was far from 'demi-Eden, other Paradise.'

Certainly this Adam out of Eden might be spared certain errors. An Adamite intelligence, in or out of the Garden, would face the facts of his environment immediately. He would not, like a subjective idealist, presume that he had made the data of his experience, nor be tempted to hypostatize his thoughts like a Hegelian. If he could be conceived as living alone (but then he would not be in our world) physical compulsions might compel him to a certain modicum of sanity in his physics, though they would not guarantee him against fantastic theological invention. Then, too, there would be no divine solicitude keeping him walled by roses from the slings and arrows of outrageous fortune. To what lengths might he not go in his impotence, ignorance, and terror? Goaded by these, he might soon generate all the magical physics, the materialistic religions, the cabalistic philosophies invented by countless noble savages in the history of civilization and countless savage philosophers in the history of thought. The pressure of noxious circumstances would soon cause him — the history of thought and the archives of primitive life bear witness — to infect his tentative readings of reality with his own hopes and fears and needs. If, as must be conceived, he is born into a world containing other beings constituted like himself, his own needs and terrors would not be the only taints upon his impartiality. He would soon be heir not only to all the actual ills, but all the traditional illusory ones of mankind. He would be prejudiced not only by his own necessities and difficulties, but by all the fixed errors and conventional anxieties which would be a part of the social environment to which he would be exposed.

A more secure example of innocence is the

Baby. The Baby is innocent, not simply in the sense that he has been uncorrupted by conventional conceptions and traditional ideals, but that his mechanisms for acquiring these are still plastic. The noble savage, after all, has conventional human intelligence. The Baby Mind, whether it be the *tabula rasa* of Locke, or the bundle of modifiable instincts of James, or the cluster of reflexes of Watson, is radically educable. He is easily, at least on paper, made over into precisely that kind of philosopher which his philosophical impresario wishes or hopes for. His innocence consists in his as yet unimpaired capacity for education. But this capacity or opportunity is not chiefly for him, but for his environment. On the basis of any psychology, sensations or instincts or original capacities or what not, the Baby is unprejudiced only in the sense that he has not yet been prejudiced. But he is impotent as to choice of which set of prejudices he shall be limited by; he is at the mercy of the society to which he happens to be born. Even his sensations of, or reactions to (as one chooses), the material world are largely modified and shifted through social agencies, language being one important modifying influence, the social attitudes of his parents and neighbors and teachers being another. He is objective only in the sense of being an object for education.

In *posse* the Baby *might* become the most detached and impartial of philosophers. In *actu*, in so far as his experience consists merely in opaque responses to his physical environment, he is not an impartial philosopher. He is no philosopher at all. He is merely that chastity of intellectual innocence out of which he will be seduced ere long. For he is all too soon initiated into categories from which he will find it impossible to escape. He must learn the grammar of some language, and some given method of thought. However lucid and pliable the grammar, however consistent and transparent the logic, they are inescapably local and provincial. A corps of philologists, physicists, and logicians might meet to create a grammar and a logic fit for a radically immediate treatment of the universe. The grammar would consist, doubtless, of a very flexible system of verbs and would eschew nouns, if it were to be a fit instrument for use in manipulation of those transiencies whose intertwinings constitute experience. The language thus deliberately created would have to be a way of expressing relations with total oblivion of their personal incidence. It would have to be a universal impartial algebra of thought. And one would have to be sure that the Baby never had a chance to hear any other language.

But assuming the Baby to be, according to the contemporary analysis of the Baby, a bundle of human capacities and desires,[1] it would be almost impossible, if not absolutely futile, to teach a vocabulary that had no words for human necessities and that was relevant to none of the compulsions of animal faith. Nor would it be of any particular use to teach a logic that had no point of human reference to a creature whose humanity inevitably determined its point of view. Only a Son of God living in the solitude of the universal could be brought up to speak a universal algebra without an accent or to display the interested *insouciance* of a god. And the only Son of God known to western tradition had his own godlike impassivity beautifully stained with human compassion.

The Baby is thus an instance of what the possibilities of objectivity are, and also what

[1] Descartes: 'Baby,' being born with innate ideas, can be dismissed as an impartial observer.

are its limits. As soon as one begins to speak, one begins to speak some particular language; as soon as one begins to think, one thinks according to some definite logic, according to a selected rationale of operation. The Logos of any particular logician must inevitably take on the clothes and coloring of some particular interest and concern. As soon as one begins to know, one knows only the knowable, that is, the discoverable and discovered conditions of the world.

Objectivity in the human sense turns out to be only a common and comparable standard of comparison; it is a social norm, not a metaphysical invariant. The Baby might in a wise community be brought up free from the most egregious superstitions, the most notorious shoddinesses of language; he might be trained to distinguish his desires from his observations and his romantic hopes from his legitimate inferences. But he would behave according to some irreducible elements of human logic and human language. He would not be able, under the freest education, to jump out of his human skin or out of the mortally experienceable realms of being. Total objectivity would be possible for him only in imagination. It would exist solely in the metaphysician's fantastic dream of what the world might look like, if there were no definite world and no definitely organized creature to apprehend it.

For pure objectivity and freedom from all prejudice one must pass from the Baby to the third instance commonly taken of the Unprejudiced Observer, the Man from Mars.

The Man from Mars is the best illustration of how philosophers have tried to jump out of their skins and out of their universe. He is, indeed, a tempting subject for speculation. If anybody could be expected to be objective, it would be a visitor from another planet. Presumably intelligent — or why else should he be invoked as an observer — he would understand the extraordinarily novel conditions of this alien earth. His observations would be keener, perhaps, than ours, and his inferences wider and more rapid, because the things about him would not yet have become a routine or his reactions to them a habit. But he would have to operate more or less within the scope of our own capacities, as a good anthropologist might try to read himself into the point of view of the savages whose methods of reasoning he was trying to study. Just how much of our logic such a visitor would find purely conventional it is difficult to tell. Contemporary physics makes it quite clear that many scientists to-day are trying desperately to take the free viewpoint of the traditional Man from Mars. They are, indeed, in the vernacular, 'trying to go him one better' and to take the point of view of the Man from Nowhere and Everywhere at once. A quotation from Eddington will illustrate how seriously the modern scientist is trying to see everything from everywhere:

We have a fairly definite idea of a normally equipt human being, and it is to his standard of appreciation that the conception of the external world of physics particularly relates. But as regards physical circumstances, it would be illogical to attach greater weight to one position, motion or size than another. We are beings who happen to be situated in a particular part of the stellar universe, compelled to journey with the motion of a rather small globe; our size is presumably regulated by the value of gravity and other physical conditions peculiar to that globe. We renounce the idea that these are physical circumstances; the purpose of conceiving an external world is to obtain a concept which could be shared by beings in any other physical circumstances whatever.

The external world is accordingly a synthesis of

appearances from all possible points of view. In the main, modern science arrives at this principle and arrives at its adopted conception of our environment by following it. The man and the microbe afford one example of the possible variety of points of view. Recently physicists have been much occupied in comparing the points of view of observers travelling with different motions, i.e., attached to different stars. The result has been entirely to revolutionize the conception of time and space in the external world. The detailed frame of time and space, in which we are accustomed to locate the events happening around us, belongs not to the external world but a particular presentation of it, namely, to those observers who are travelling with the same velocity as ourselves, as the earth. A being on a different star with a different reckoning of time and space, and his location of external events would be a distorted version of our own. Man is not in the habit of taking trips to other stars, so the corresponding synthesis has been left to scientific research.[1]

The Man from Mars is, of course, compelled during his sojourn among us to take our physical point of view, assuming always that his own physical and mental organization is sufficiently analogous to our own to make that possible.

[1] (Slightly abridged from Arthur S. Eddington's essay on 'The Domain of Physical Science,' in *Science, Religion, and Reality*.)

But the assumptions of Euclidean geometry and Newtonian science would seem to him no more eternal, external, or universally compulsive than the custom of eating recently slain grandmothers would appear so to the missionary.

There would be a central and profound sense in which the Man from Mars would be objective, and that would be in the sphere of morals. Just as for him, no physical point of view could be 'right' or 'wrong,' so all moral viewpoints would be relative in a more thoroughgoing sense than they are even to the emancipated earthly philosopher. For behind all pleas for the recognition of the relativity of moral standards, lurks always some assumption about the unquestionableness of human good. From the scepticism of Protagoras or Hume, to the pragmatism of Dewey, all relativists in morals have had some more or less friendly axe to grind. They have always been motivated by some deeply felt, though not always clearly conceived, standard of human good.

The Man from Mars, unless he be conceived as unimaginably solar in his sympathies, could not be expected to take any variety of human good as his ultimate criterion. He might simply for the satisfaction of curiosity (though that is a human trait he might not share) be interested to observe the way all things with us had a human slant, from physics to morals, from politics to metaphysics. Himself free from any susceptibility to human values, he might be nothing but amused by the most serious of our moral systems and ideals. Their intensity would constitute for him their quaintness. 'What droll perspectives,' he might say to himself, 'are held by these midgets on a tiny planet, who are able to see even uncaring eternity only in terms of their agitated little selves.' His own provincialism might be evidenced in the fact that for a long time he would find it impossible to take anything but a Martian viewpoint, however that happened to be defined. Our tenderest maxims and softest Christian moralities might appear to him as inverted and gruesome as the bloody sacrifices to a sun god appear to the civilized observer. The whole human conception of morals might be impossible for him to comprehend. Being an unusually travelled solar citizen, he might envisage the possibility of a solar point of view. Like M. Briand, who claimed at Locarno to have learned to speak European, he might have learned to think in truly cosmic terms. In his freedom from prepossession it might be possible for him to conceive a point of view more radically universal even than that of the solar system. He might in a far vaster sense than Parmenides learn to think of the All and the One, to dream of 'a synthesis of all possible points of view.'

If he were inclined to be philosophical — and the radical novelties to which he was exposed might, indeed, provoke him to speculation — he might wander up and down the earth for a space, hoping to find some philosopher approaching himself in objectivity. It is tantalizing to think where he might find such a one. Certainly it would not be among those who take human good as the central canon of their thought. He would be too genuine and too genial a cosmopolitan for that. Nor would he find much more completeness and freedom among those who took physics as a serious transcript of reality. He would see, as few human beings can, that physics is, after all, human, that it is a selective structure of operations, just as morals is a selective organon of desires. In point of emancipation, the physicist who turned his physics into an ultimate metaphysics would appear no more emancipated than a moralist who turned his system or programme of prejudices into a tablet of divine commands. It would be easy to show the futility of taking even human happiness with cosmic seriousness. It would be not much harder to show the absurdity of taking time and space and the conventionally external world as ultimate.

In time, doubtless — for while he lived on earth he would have to act as if he believed in time — he might discover that his living here had corrupted his own objectivity, or revealed to him that it had never existed. For he would come to realize that his spirit, while it was free from human passions and prejudices, had passions and prejudices a-plenty of its own. What would his thirst for objectivity be but a thirst for a wider range for the body's fortune, a hunger for a more various and complete subject matter of discourse? The Man from Mars might ultimately realize that he would have to be the Spirit of the whole universe to comprehend its fullness of integrity. And then he would still be the spirit *of* the universe, not a spirit outside it. He might even give up the vain and wonderful delusion of being a free mind, of seeing everything steadily and seeing it whole. He might recognize that he was the Man from Mars, but that he was a Man, and that Mars was only one among many stars and Martian philosophy only one among many stellar perspectives.

For the Man from Mars is not truly detached, since his Mind is the Mind of some being, with definite interests and a definite point of view, however broad those interests may be, or however that point of view be defined. He is living in *some* envisaged world, however much larger it be than the provinces of earth, or the jurisdiction of human concerns.

It turns out, therefore, upon examination that Adam is innocent completely only when he is living in a perfect and innocuous Eden. He is a clear observer of a scene in which there are no humans but Eve to observe. The Man from Mars is only in degree less provincial than the human beings whom he studies. His detachment is mostly irony, the irony of a passing foreigner among a race who seem to take their internal politics too seriously, and who convert their local map into a universal topography. The Baby is plastic, but his plasticity is fated always to be a special inescapable mould.

Surely if these hypothetical observers be found, on analysis, to be poor examples of innocence, plasticity, and detachment, no mere human philosopher, civilized, earthly, and adult, can hope to regard himself as genuinely impartial. In essence God (a transcendent, not an immanent God) would be the only truly detached observer. And even God in most theologies is prejudiced in the interests of his mortal children. He speaks their own infant language and governs his universe in terms of their childish and earthly whims. Aristotle's God may be excepted. For his thoughts are the expressions of the fruits and harmonies of all things. But in Aristotle the Absolute Thinker has his existence exhaustively defined in his Absolute thoughts, and these thoughts are not really absolute, for they are merely the music made by one out of any number of conceivable worlds.

Adam, the Baby, and the Man from Mars have always been invoked as the only three unprejudiced observers of the human scene. They will not do. No one will. Not even God who is always the God of one kind of realm only among an infinity of thinkable ones.

That is a lesson for all hasty philosophers to

contemplate before they speak of the last analysis, or presume in the auto-intoxication of their own words, that their vision is a transcript of the Absolute.

TOWARD A PHILOSOPHY OF CRITICISM

OUR MEN OF LETTERS AND OUR MEN OF THOUGHT

THE relations between imaginative literature and speculative thought have always been obscure, and never more so than in our own day. It is impossible to read more than ten pages of Virginia Woolf, Thomas Mann, Aldous Huxley, Zona Gale, Willa Cather, T. S. Eliot, to mention only a few, without realizing that these so different writers are in varying degrees touched and controlled by the drift, the perplexity and the excitement of contemporary thought. Nearly all those mentioned are directly or implicitly concerned with general ideas; nearly all of them are predominantly occupied with at least one ultimate idea, the state of the soul in the contemporary scene, the plight and prospect of the spirit of the world. And that plight and prospect they see inevitably in terms fixed by the unembroidered speculations of thinkers in this and the last generation. Some of them, notably Thomas Mann and Aldous Huxley, by a different turn of their careers, might have been professional philosophers. If philosophy be defined as the love of wisdom and the vision of the Good Life, then some of them, like Willa Cather in her compassionate serenity, are more genuinely philosophers than those professionally labeled as such.

It is impossible, on the other hand, to have even a cursory acquaintance with the speculation of such men as Whitehead, Dewey, Santayana, with the new physics and the current ferment in psychology, without realizing the profound infiltration of these enterprises of thought into the enterprises of literary art. They have affected the content and brought a new cosmos and a complex dark soul into contemporary fiction. They have brought a lyric irony and a self-sceptical passion into poetry. They have affected the method. The static photographs of things seen in deathlike arrest have been replaced, in Joyce, in Virginia Woolf, in Dorothy Richardson, by a moving picture of the living stream of consciousness, the intimate flow of experience itself, of which Bergson was the revealer in philosophy.

It does not matter that some writers affected by the current ferment are swimming, like Sherwood Anderson, in waters obviously too deep for them. It does not matter that many a minor philosophical poet has never read the work of a major philosopher. There is what Whitehead calls a 'climate of opinion.' Winds of doctrine play over the minds of even the most indolently attentive literary artists. Even when the writer turns away from ideas to 'life,' he is bound to regard life in terms of, or, as Mr. Edwin Muir points out, in opposition to the terms of the Zeitgeist, the complex of moods and ideas current in his age. Consciously or unconsciously, angrily or acquiescently, the writer's voice is not his alone. Plato says somewhere that God took away the minds of poets that they might express his. Writers may not be primarily concerned with ideas; they may, like D. H. Lawrence, fear mind and all its works; but the ideas of an age speak through them none the less.

Ideas, of course, do not speak in their unmitigated and pure accents in belles-lettres. For a creative writer is concerned not with what ideas signify to the analytical mind, but what they are as vivid immediacies to the constructive imagination. The novelist is concerned with ideas only in so far as they are lived, exemplified, touched by the characters in his created little cosmos; the poet in so far as they are the sustaining mood, the essential theme of the music of his poem. That is why H. G. Wells, for all his newsy intellectual alertness, is a negligible voice of the spirit of his age. He is a busy amateur sociologist, a quick memorizer of the newest jargon of ideas; the concepts with which he is dealing have not become woven into the texture of his characters. The sex-life and the sociology of 'William Clissold' have very little to do with each other. That is why Virginia Woolf, who in her novels never discusses a theory, nevertheless sounds the true cadence of the current mind. The hum of consciousness, the flow of time (the stuff and matrix of experience itself as understood by contemporary thought) are in these pages. And opposite, too, is the brooding hunger for beauty and peace and fulfillment amid chaos and distraction that possesses Mrs. Dalloway, the beating awareness of her heart on that crystal London afternoon in June of time that washes away all hopes and frustrations and fulfillments alike. Mrs. Ramsaye in 'To the Lighthouse,' amid the trivia of her family, externally busy with the passing and the tawdry and the infelicitous absurdities of the daily round, has a haunting, persistent com-

pulsion by unassuageable beauty. All of this
moves on fluently like that stream of consciousness that James was first to talk of in philosophy, the very simulacrum of that 'pure experience' which is for John Dewey the matrix
of all action and thought. There is the inter-
play throughout Mrs. Woolf's novels of personalities not by what they do in the clear daylight of their deliberate awareness, but what
they love and hate and hope for in the dark
forest shadows of the unconscious. All this is
the fruit of a mind singularly and subtly alive
to the temper of contemporary thinking, aware
of it not in its abstraction but flowing as it were
in the life blood of contemporary human
beings.

There are, of course, between the speculative thinkers and the imaginative writers,
liaison officers in the persons of the more
speculative critics. There is to-day a group
of interpreters in this country, Van Wyck
Brooks, Lewis Mumford, Joseph Wood Krutch,
and Edmund Wilson (a year ago the list would
have been led by Stuart Sherman), Edwin
Muir in England, Paul Valéry in France, who
are writing, on the one hand, of a passionate
acquaintance with life and letters, on the other

hand, out of a deep, dispassionate concern with the method underlying a point of view or a method in literature. They attempt not simply to point our surface beauties and agilities, but to examine, lay bare and estimate the assumptions which underlie a writer's sympathies and aversions and determine his methods and his problems.

Of these Paul Valéry is probably the most comprehensive and speculative. In the great tradition of French philosophical criticism of literature in a time not peculiarly metaphysical, he daringly reasserts the importance of considering fundamentals in and behind a work of art. He is in essence calling to a common council the workers in thought and the workers in belles-lettres who have hitherto kept to their own narrowing compartments. There is a persuasive grandeur about his conception of 'l'homme universel,' the ideal modern Leonardo, who shall be at once poet and scientist, prophet and saint, whose wide art will be the expression of an almost geometric comprehension of things. Edwin Muir, less preoccupied with general philosophical ideas on their own account, has a gift, notably exemplified in 'Transition,' for elucidating in such writers as

D. H. Lawrence, James Joyce, and T. S. Eliot, the cardinal presumptions they are implicitly making, the cardinal doctrines they are implicitly teaching. One need not risk very much in suggesting that this young critic has in his two books, 'Latitudes' and 'Transition,' said more that was to the point concerning the ideas in and behind contemporary literature than almost any critic writing in English. It might appear that it was among these liaison officers that one could best study the curious relations between ideas in their bare analytic essence and ideas in their imaginative realization. These men bring to bear upon contemporary literature almost an expert's acquaintance with the outlines of contemporary thought. But what interests a lover of literature is not what ideas a critic brings to it, but what ideas have been woven into its fiber and tissue. How far, in short, has contemporary thought affected the contemporary imagination?

A just and common observation made upon contemporary literature is that the dominant mood in its serious practitioners is one of irony and disillusion. Mr. Aldous Huxley with his half insouciant, half tormented analysis of love into hormones and idealisms of all sorts, into biological compulsions or evasions, is a case in point. The whole bleak, uncaring world that 'science reveals for our belief' is supposed to find in him its elegant disillusioned spokesman.

Mr. Huxley is a primary illustration of the way in which ideas pass from speculation to literature. Not only do they appear less purely; they appear less promptly in the latter. Much of the atmosphere of disillusion in contemporary writing is a weary reflex to the post-war period, an affectation of smartness or wistfulness, or a permanent motif of the frail minor poet in the brutal major world. But in so far as it is intellectual in character (as it is in Mr. Huxley) it is a belated literary reaction to what was going on in late nineteenth-century thought rather than to what is going on in our own. Mr. Huxley is responding to the world of his grandfather, Thomas Henry Huxley, rather than to the living currents of speculation. That 'alien' world about which Mr. Huxley and Anatole France and T. S. Eliot are in different ways concerned is a nightmare inferred from the mathematico-physical world of Newton and the mechanical biology of Darwin, which constituted a dogma among the emancipates by the end of the nineteenth century.

In that alien world all that men held dear and beautiful had no status or significance. Our little raptures are the foolish complications of bio-chemistry; our illusions and dis-illusions are meaningless in a meaningless world. 'Only on the firm foundation of un-yielding despair,' cried Bertrand Russell melo-dramatically in 'The Free Man's Worship,' 'can the soul's habitation henceforth be safely built.'

Literary men have been suffering from this nightmare of the alien world for the last fifty years. Thomas Hardy makes it his major theme and gives it majestic finality. Anatole France found an anodyne against it in irony and pity. Aldous Huxley, young, dapperly fitted out with a more recent technical jargon of science and a more fashionable list of despair-ing modern follies, has the same bleak cosmos as his theater.

In one way or another much contemporary literature has been trying to face or trying to flee this unamiable setting. D. H. Lawrence has tried to escape it by running away from the intellect that recognizes it, returning to, rely-ing on the mentality of the Bushman and the dark magic of the soul, seeking healing communication by passion rather than the certain misunderstandings and despairs of thought. Joyce has tried to face the world with a Gargantuan irony. He has reveled bitterly in a minutely recorded horror, reporting without compunction the dunglike realities the soaring soul finds in its own flesh and in the earth it inhabits. T. S. Eliot has found half-adjustment, half-escape in exploring subtly the paradox of the mind listening to its own frustrations in the *Wasteland* of the age. Some, like Romain Rolland, have found the soul's safety in the retreat of Art. H. G. Wells has whistled Progress via Intelligence on his penny whistle trying to drown the strident voices of chaos.

But it is not merely the blind mechanistic cosmos with which the sad-eyed or skeptical men of letters have been trying to make some peace or from which they have been trying to find some refuge. They have been escaping, too, from the Machine Age. Not only is the nature of things fatal and rigid, but civilization is becoming so, too, and making likewise — in how many poems and novels and essays have we heard it — the nature of man. Sherwood

Anderson looks away with pitying distaste
from a 'standardized' world to one where individual craftsmanship, 'the workman playing
with his materials,' will be the reassertion of
the soul in a society of automata. 'Some day,'
he writes in that biographical credo, 'The
Story Teller's Story,' 'the workmen will come
back to their materials out of the sterile land
of standardization. The day of the rediscovery
of man by man may not be so far off as we
imagine.' Galsworthy yearns, in the preface to
'The Forsyte Saga,' with not too much hope,
that the spirit of Possession may yield to the
spirit of Beauty. D. H. Lawrence moves from
the gray leveling compulsions of modernity to
the primitive in thought and life and emotion.
Sinclair Lewis escapes into invective and satire.
Yeats turns his back on it all and finds his
escape in a world of mystics and fairies. Elinor
Wylie moves in an exquisite saving phantasy
of an enameled eighteenth century; Cabell in a
mythical mediæval Poictesme.

The mechanistic world and the Machine
Age have distressed our writers, and few have
been conscious that mechanistic science may
be less final and damning, the Machine Age less
eternal or fatal than they had imagined. While

the 'alien world' has been the theme of endless novels and poems, the philosophy which
emerges in the picture and heartbreak of the
alien world has been breaking up. The mechanistic cosmos, colorless of value and indifferent to human concerns, has, it must be remembered, been built intellectually only these
last three hundred years. The realm of beauty
and wonder, tenderness and worship, which is
the world of imagination, has been building up
for ten thousand. It is no wonder that it is
only in the last fifty years that 'black' science
has hypnotized, almost morbidly hypnotized
the imaginations of our writers, not that they
have found a bitter incongruity between the
brutal mathematical indifference of nature and
the frail, doomed aspirations of man.

But during the last fifty years much has been
happening to that alleged ultimate science to
which literary men have responded with irony
or flight. The concern of the serious writer is
obviously with the spirit of man. And the
spirit has apparently been lost in the eyes of
modern speculation. It is conditioned by its
animal body, limited by the mechanisms of
nature and crushed by the regimentation of the
machine.

Meanwhile any reader of Einstein or Whitehead or Eddington knows in general what has been happening. The bleak world in which the spirit has no home has been breaking up. That clear, fatal system of mathematically certain, morally meaningless physics has been shown to be a huge and questionable intellectual abstraction. From the point of view of ultimacy it is indeed become almost a huge joke. Whitehead says in 'Science and the Modern World,' a book whose revolutionary import is only gradually being realized:

The progress of science now has reached a turning point. The stable foundations of physics have broken up.... The old foundations of scientific thought are becoming unintelligible. Time, space, matter, ether, electricity, mechanism, organism, configuration, structure, pattern, organization, all require reinterpretation. What is the use talking about a mechanical explanation when you do not know what you mean by mechanics?

It is impossible here to go into any detail of the transformation which is overtaking science. But its essence may be stated as follows: The crude materialism and mechanism which is what with many literary men passes for Science is passing away. The simple old-fashioned mechanism of matter in motion is no longer in any sense ultimate. Space and time themselves that loomed so final are now seen to be complex functions of a highly abstract intellectualism. Æsthetic and moral goods which seemed to the old-fashioned materialism of the nineteenth century to be helpless obbligati in the realities revealed by science, are seen to be as much a part of Reality as sticks and stones and atoms and centers of force. Reality, if it is anywhere, is where the human imagination has always instinctively found it, in the simple totality of an actual and concrete moment, in the event that the human spirit in its breathing being lives.

Nor is it necessary for literary men to flee in imagination from the Machine Age. There are indeed symptoms that they are ceasing to do so. The literary imagination is nourished on a literary tradition, and it has been taught by the poetry and fiction of the past to find nourishment on the beauty of a mediæval cathedral or guild, rather than to see it in the actual towering beauties and possibilities of beauty that a Machine Age makes possible. The Machine may come to seem the servant and instrument of human intelligence, the emancipator, not the murderer of the spirit. The spirit, after all, lives in a body and must make itself at home in the world. The Machine is simply a more complex and adroit and far-reaching hand. It need not be the Frankenstein monster that slays us. Aldous Huxley in India came to the conclusion that sanitation and machines might better nourish the spirit than all the ethereal spiritual doctrines of the East.

Men of letters are naturally concerned with the life and career of the spirit in the world. Part of their perplexity and part of their frustration has come from a sense that the world as it is known and the age as it is lived inevitably shatter the spirit or corrupt its purity. They have doubted even that the life of the spirit is anything but a sweet delusion that our acid insights will no longer permit us to solace ourselves by. There are beginning to be signs on the literary horizon that a new spirituality is coming into letters, nourished on no illusions and depressed by no anachronistic nightmares. The 'universal man' that Valéry speaks of has not yet arisen. But an indication of what he would be like is suggested in Thomas Mann, whose magnificent work, 'The Magic Mountain,' is the testament of a singularly comprehensive mind moving with passion through the whole circle of modern emotions and ideas. His hero, a tuberculosis patient on a high mountain resort in Switzerland, in the long, sad leisure of an illness that cuts him off from the flatland, has time to consider closely the relation of Body and Spirit, of Time and Eternity, of Passion and Thought as they exhibit themselves in the lives of his fevered companions and in the fevers of our time. There is more than a taint of decay about the huge work; Mann, too, has the modern tragic feeling that we are encased in the body of this death, that life itself is from the point of view of pure spirit, a kind of disease, a corruption and a death. His hero, in his colloquies with himself, with a passionate Italian disciple of Reason, and a fanatic Jesuit supporter of mysticism and other worldliness, canvasses almost every question that has tormented the modern consciousness. Spiritually speaking, however, the climax of the book is in the vision Hans Castrorp has during a blinding snow storm on a wild mountain where he has gone skiing. It is a reverie compacted of thought done into images, the reverie of a soul that has been through every disillusion, through the mirage of time itself to a vision of a clear, gracious and ordered humanity, 'a mutual courteous regard of the children of the sun.' He sees a fair, almost idyllic people atoning by their high dignity of love and reason the 'blood sacrifice,' the suffering horror that lies at the basis of all beauty.

There are writers, nearer home, too, who are beginning to come into the sunlight out of the recesses and glooms which a hasty and precocious intellectualism has taught them. A little poem that appeared some time ago in 'The Nation' sums up with avid beauty the substance of negative feeling that is beginning to be the furniture of a past epoch. It is 'The Corrosive Season,' by Lynn Riggs, and its essence is in these lines:

> If we have demanded this corrosive season,
> Of drought, if we have bent,
> Backward from the plow asking
> Even less than is sent,
>
> Surely we may be no bitterer
> Than the shrunk grape,
> Clinging to the wasted stem
> It cannot escape.

TOWARD A PHILOSOPHY OF
CRITICISM

A LITERARY critic, when he is anything more than a book reviewer, is a philosopher. To criticize a book is to estimate a world, though it be only one created in imagination. To estimate a world is to have or to imply certain bases of belief about its nature, its movement and its destiny. But a literary critic is often both ignorant that he is and unwilling to be a philosopher. The beliefs which make him hail a novel or a book of poetry as good or bad are often presumptions of which he is quite unaware. His intellectual foundations come from current science and philosophy and from an intellectual tradition which he himself, accustomed chiefly to read literature, does not know at first hand. It requires a Sainte-Beuve or a Taine to be radically aware of the presumptions on which his criticism is based. Only in a first-rate mind are prejudices examined in the light of principles. Only in a first-rate mind are there the honesty and ability to come to grips with first principles at all. There are not enough first-rate minds to go around, nor are all of them engaged in literary criticism. Critics are, moreover, almost desperately unwilling to be philosophers. The literary critic, himself the defeated half of an artist, has the artist's plausible contempt for general ideas. He tries, rather, as Pater tried, to render himself the voice, intimate and sympathetic, of the work of the artist himself, to catch the writer, as it were, in his habit and gesture, to be an organ of appreciation, not an arbiter of praise or blame, or not an intellect disciplined to fundamental analysis. As a result, the average literary critic, even one of taste and cultivation, eschews either the examination or the enunciation of a general view of life or a basic conception of social order. He is constantly implying a science which he does not know or understand, a metaphysics which he could not expound or perhaps agree to, and a social philosophy whose origins he does not suspect and whose consequences he might, if he were faced with them, scarcely admit. His prejudices lie deeper than he realizes, and they are often in no honest sense his own.

Literary critics in our generation are being forced, despite themselves, to be philosophers, though poor ones, for the materials of current literature are becoming increasingly provocative of philosophical consideration. One cannot possibly examine the work of a writer like Marcel Proust without being provoked to a consideration of the whole meaning of time and implication of memory. To read Virginia Woolf is to move into that whole realm of modern thought in which reality is conceived of as a flux and life itself as a duration, troubled and prospective and uncertain. To read Joyce is to be brought face to face with that changing order of scientific conception in which the whole of experience becomes bound together, for all its miscellany, into one organic whole. Among American writers, to read Willa Cather is to read an appreciation of a past, an implied arraignment of a present American civilization.

To follow Sinclair Lewis is to read an indictment of our established complacencies. Again, to delight in the poetry of T. S. Eliot is to delight among other things, sardonically, in the indictment, cryptic and chiseled, of a waste land of a world. And among those writers who are trying to retreat from speculation or criticism or sociology to an art as timeless as it is exquisite, the critic discerns once again those underlying questions of the relation of the artist to ideas and to morals, of the function of literature in society. The writers, themselves only half consciously philosophers, are driving the critics once again to philosophy. Just as the bristling philosophical implications of current literature are tempting the academic philosophers, as in Van Metre Ames's 'Æsthetics of the Novel,' to literary criticism.

In looking over the table of current criticism, it is hard to find any one more completely metaphysical in character than Paul Valéry. One is indeed tempted to suspect that Paul Valéry is a philosopher who, by some seduction on the way, came to live with literature, and for longer than he intended. In his attempt to reduce criticism to a kind of geometry, and to make his ideal of a literary man an artistic expression of a wide and comprehensive scientific truth, Paul Valéry reveals the bias of the metaphysician rather than the interest of the literary man. Even his doctrine of 'pure poetry' is almost a doctrine of pure mathematics, and in attempting to reduce literature to its metaphysical fundamentals, he has almost deserted letters for pure metaphysics. But Paul Valéry is at least indicating an attempt as resolute as

297

it is, in this generation, a novelty, to go back to fundamentals, to enunciate a frank set of first principles, instead of merely implying a concealed set of prejudices. One may quarrel on a dozen grounds with his doctrine of the universal man, the man of letters who shall be the Leonardo of the present age, turning his informed and exact vision of the world into imaginative beauty. Grand and impressive as is such a function for a writer, there are others no less attractive if less noble. Our age may cry aloud as Mr. Scott Buchanan says in his recent book, 'Possibility,' for a poet to do for the modern version of Nature what Lucretius did for the ancient and Dante for the mediæval world. Even so. But the minor artist, who wishes to do nothing but render with gayety or poetic fidelity some section of current manners or some eternal section of life, also has his rights and his public. Literature has a license to be a carnival as well as a discourse. M. Paul Valéry is too much engaged in discourse to remember that this is so. But he is reminding us of what the minor artist forgets, that the major artist has always had a vision, and sometimes one no less wide than the world.

The late Stuart Sherman (since sometimes

the best place to go for living voices is to the dead) took the standpoint of the generous minded moralist rather than of the scientist and metaphysician. He represented the point of view, shared to some extent by Mr. Lewis Mumford, and stemming rather directly from Matthew Arnold, that all literature, like poetry, was a criticism of life, and that criticism of literature was therefore a criticism of life also. It was for this reason that in the earlier years of his writing he condemned novelists like Theodore Dreiser and Sherwood Anderson, who represented to him, as to Irving Babbitt, the enemies of reason and order and repose, the canons of the classic tradition. It was on moral grounds, too, when fulness of life rather than discipline and restraint became his criterion, that he began to welcome the new writers. Were they not, he pointed out in 'Critical Woodcuts,' indicating in the imaginative experiments of fiction new avenues of spontaneity, new ways of life?

Among the moralists, too, may be included Mr. Lewis Mumford, a reformer with his earnest eye fixed upon beauty. He measures American life and American letters by the extent to which both have the freedom and grace of art.

His praises and indictments seem both to flow
from a moral conception that salvation lies in
pagan freedom, a freedom whose one discipline
is that of art and whose one willing responsi-
bility that of creation. 'The Golden Day' is a
passionate piece of retrospection toward the
bright spaciousness of Emerson's day and viewpoint, an arraignment of current life and letters
because they have lost the heritage of a freedom at once rich and simple. Our instrumen-
talism, the ugly insignificance of our doings
and our environment are all destroyers of life
and corrupters of letters. Mr. Mumford is
constantly implying that the simplification
and enrichment of both will go hand in hand.

There are critics, too, preoccupied neither
with metaphysics nor morals, but with an attempt to discern in current writing the psychological motives which that writing connotes, to
indicate, without preference or contempt, the
ideas or the impulses which they involve.
Edwin Muir, in 'Transition'; Joseph Wood
Krutch in his critical articles in 'The Nation';
Dorothy Brewster and John Burrell in their
neglected 'Dead Reckonings in Fiction,' have,
all of them, tried to explore those recesses of
feeling and of subconscious intention which

animate the current literary scene. They have
been concerned with the agonies, hungers and
ideas which go into contemporary fiction. It
may be objected, and with some justice, that
the business of the critic is the business of
æsthetic analysis; his problems are those of any
other literary artist, the problems of imagination trying to find for itself a form and a
language. It is a perversion of literature and
of criticism to turn the attention of the writer
and reader from the eternal problems and endless delights of a gay or moving art, to the
interests, secondary and periphrastic, of the
moralist, the psycho-analyst and the metaphysician.

The objection would be well sustained if
current literature had not itself widened its
boundaries so that its themes, in its major
practitioners, involved ideas and ranges of
emotion and moral problems that have never
before entered into fiction. André Gide, concerned to a high degree of purity with technique, is moving into provinces of the soul
that have only recently entered into letters.
Thomas Mann has created a whole gallery of
living creatures (no one will ever forget the
author or the little boy in 'Death in Venice,'

and in Switzerland around every bend in a mountain road one expects to come upon half the patients in that cure of bodies and souls which is the sanitorium in 'The Magic Mountain').

But Thomas Mann has done more than bring to life the denizens of a world. He has made them the voices of almost all the ideas with which the contemporary intellectual imagination has been concerned. Every serious portrait of life in our generation carries persuasion or condemnation with it. Even the artist, fleeing from the world about him or the tumults within him to realms of fantasy or nonsense, is, in his flight, making a judgment and a commentary upon the scene which his eyes have turned in fear or disillusion.

One might say, indeed, that the most surprising felicity in psychological insight has come from the novelists rather than from the psychologists. Not all the laboratory apparatus or intelligence tests of the last decade have given more insight into the life, tortuous and complex, of the moving and remembering psyche, than Proust does in a few chapters of 'Swann's Way.' Not all the discussion of the relation of body and spirit among the philosophers gives us so near a sense of their implication as is rendered in their involvement, as monstrous as it is plausible, in the lewd and lyric pages of Joyce.

Nor are professional moralists more bitterly or devotedly concerned with morals than many contemporary novelists. No ethical condemnation of American materialism and complacent efficiency has come more clearly from any moralist than has come from the unedifying reports of Sinclair Lewis. No more compelling plea for a richer way of life has come from any preachment than rises from the commentary, serene but intense, implied in the novels of Zona Gale or Willa Cather.

There are bright young critics arising who plead for a pure and abstract art of fiction, as there are painters who plead for an art of pure and abstract design. 'Let us forget the meaning of life and its machinery,' we are asked by the lovers of a purist literature, 'let us render only the essence of its moments and its conflicts, poetic and eternal.'

Whether painting can be an art of absolute and pure design is an open question. But that literature could, or should, would certainly appear to be less clear. The instruments of literature are words, and words, though one be arrested by their music, have meanings as well as vibrations. Literature, that is to say, has a subject matter, the human consciousness. And into that contemporary human psyche have entered of late sensations and probings that inevitably make the serious novelists and poets of our day metaphysicians, moralists, and psychologists, none the less so because their discourse is drama rather than analysis.

A serious criticism will have to be educated to something more than literary surfaces. It will have to become aware of those currents of thought, coming from the laboratory and the study and the clinic, which are gradually transforming the contemporary consciousness itself. The critic who confines himself to pure literature will find that literature has itself become impure, that it has got itself richly tangled up and corrupted by the whole self-conscious complexity of modern experience. While the critics remain for the most part, for money or amusement, concerned with the prattle of the literary shop, the writers are growing up. They are dealing with subtler recesses and realities of the educated and understanding. The writers are trying to understand life. It remains only for the critics to understand literature.